I'M NOT A PSYCHOLOGIST BUT I DO HAVE A PHD IN MOTHERHOOD

I'M NOT A PSYCHOLOGIST BUT I DO HAVE A PHD IN MOTHERHOOD

A MOTHER'S GUIDE TO PARENTING

Norma Gindi

I'm Not a Psychologist But I Do Have a PhD in Parenting/Norma Gindi —1st edition

Edited by Matthew Gilbert

ISBN: 9798722489661

Contents

Dedication

To my children:

Vivian—my pride
Frieda—my light
Eddy—my love
Ronnie—my joy

My whole heart . . .

To Zac:

"Who am I without you by my side?"
—George Harrison (from *What Is Life*)

Introduction

My mother's voice rings through me every time I face a difficulty. I see her proud eyes every time I look in the mirror. Her warmth envelopes me when I hug my own children.

I was fortunate to grow up in a happy home where my siblings and I were loved unconditionally. My mother's compassion and gentle touch have always been and continue to be a model for me. I also love helping people and being socially invested—a passion I inherited from my father. Although my upbringing was full of good times, we had our fair share of difficulties and challenges, like any family. Ironically though, those challenges taught me a great deal about life. My parents' response to life's ups and downs paved the way for a purposeful perspective on my own journey.

I was born and raised in a small Jewish community in Brooklyn where family and friends continue to be my support system. After high school, I went to the Fashion Institute of Technology in New York City to study fashion merchandising, but I didn't really know what I wanted to be. I was attending college when I met my husband. We started a family and were blessed with four children: Vivian, Frieda, Eddy, and Ronnie.

My passion for parenting was sparked by taking parenting classes with Mrs. Esther Tawachi. In fact, I took those classes for over ten years and became known as "Esther T's student." When Esther couldn't be reached, people would call me for advice about their children. Over time, by word of mouth, people would refer me to their friends, parents, and siblings. During this time, I formed many relationships within the community. At times I didn't even know who I was speaking to, but it didn't matter. I love helping people, expanding my knowledge, and seeing things through. Along the way, I realized I have a knack for understanding children and getting to the root of a problem.

During my free time, I read parenting books, psychology books, and articles about psychology. I have watched every Oprah, Dr. Phil, and Supernanny episode on television. It's safe to say that all roads have been pointing in this direction. I don't have all the answers, but I don't think anyone else does either. Nevertheless, I have a lot to say on parenting, which explains this book.

My husband has always been my biggest fan. He has and continues to be my compass. I've had countless conversations with him about my "itch"—or, as he refers to it, my "calling"—to explore my passion for parenting. He suggested that I start writing down some notes after every parenting call about the topic discussed. Soon after he came up with the idea of turning my notes into a book. We both laughed at the thought. He said even if it took ten years to complete, it would be a healthy outlet for me. Two months later the book was done. Did I mention I have a lot to say about parenting?

The focus of this book is to help all parents, or soon to be parents, learn the basic building blocks of parenthood. It is not a prescriptive guide but rather a compass for navigating those sometimes choppy waters. It provides skills and practical tips that are crucial for building relationships with your children that will minimize conflict and inappropriate behavior while harnessing their innate abilities and unique personalities.

Note: At times I refer to Judaic traditions and principles that are important to my family. I'm sure you have your own.

This book is my diary, and it comes straight from my heart. I hope it touches yours!

PART I: THE BIG PICTURE

1

The Why

Ever wonder why you parent the way you do? How you got to where you are in your parenting approach? Have you noticed similarities—or intentional differences—in the way you parent your children compared to the way you were parented? How conscious are you of your parenting approach?

As a mother of four, I remember dreaming about my first baby. What would he be like? Who would he look like? Would he have blue eyes like my mother-in-law? Become a dentist like my father-in-law? I figured he'd be athletic like my father. When my doctor called out, "It's a girl!", I knew this would only be the first of many surprises.

As parents, we dream of our children before they are born. We wonder what they'll be like and what they'll become. Actual parenthood, however, has a funny way of transforming these self-centered ideals into selfless reality. We discover that our journey through parenthood not only influences our children's growth but also takes us as parents on our own path of learning and self-development.

Self-reflection has a way of intensifying when we become parents. It turns out that much of our parenting approach stems not only from our own childhood experiences but also how we responded to those experiences, and it's important to realize that. Reflecting on your childhood experiences can help you become more aware of how you react toward your own children and why you use that approach. For example, sometimes you might hear yourself talk to or yell at your kids the way your parents did with you. It's hard to believe we need to call on our past to become better parents in the present, but the more conscious you are of how you parent your children and where some of those patterns may have originated, the better you can support your children, and the more likely they will blossom into their best selves.

A mother once lamented to me that her three-year-old daughter wouldn't clean up during clean-up time in school. I asked her how clean-up time goes at home. "My mother was a neat freak who made us treat our home like a museum," she replied, "and I will not do that to my own children." That was an "Aha!" moment for me, and soon it became one for her. This mother's childhood experiences deeply affected how she parented her child. To be clear, her approach had little to do with the fact that her own mother was neat; it had a lot more to do with her *reaction* to her mother's parenting style.

It is not uncommon to parent in the opposite way that you were parented, and it's certainly not uncommon to follow in your parents' footsteps. The problem is that when we adopt these approaches— sometimes unconsciously—we aren't considering the child or children we are parenting. When we aren't conscious of our children's needs and personalities, we typically revert back to our past as a point of parenting reference, whether by re-enacting the parenting experiences that made us feel good or avoiding the difficulties we experienced. In so doing, we are essentially parenting *ourselves*. When we don't consider the individual children we are raising, we won't be able to meet their needs. More importantly, we won't be able to help them on their journey through life.

So, how do you break the embedded patterns of your past and parent your children according to their needs, not yours? The process looks like this:

- Be conscious of your past experiences.
- Be present with your children to learn about their true essence.
- Be open to supporting them on their own unique path.

Adopting healthy affirmations that see your children as individuals, such as "I am not my parents" and "My children are not me," can be helpful. By seeing your children with fresh eyes, you can begin to focus on their individual needs.

It is also essential to believe that, as parents, we are the best fit for our children, capable of providing them with the tools they need to succeed in life. One statement that I hear a lot is, "My children deserve a better mother." "Mom guilt" is real, and it can be emotionally consuming. It's important to want to grow as a person, but you will struggle to grow as a parent if you are unable to accept yourself.

When I'm dealing with mom guilt, I go to the following healthy affirmations:

- "I make mistakes, but it's OK."
- "I lost my cool, but I recognize it and will become more conscious of my behavior in the future."
- "My daughter acts like me when I get mad, but she is not me. I will be more conscious of modeling healthy coping skills in the future."
- "I allowed my ego to get in the way of effective parenting, but I recognize it, and that's what's important."
- "I could have been more present with my children today, but things come up, and I will be more present tomorrow."
- "I am not perfect, but I am enough."

It's also important to recognize what negative self-talk looks like:

- "I am the worst mom."
- "I'm never going to change."
- "He's going to turn out just like me."
- "My kids deserve better."

Negative self-talk keeps us from reaching our potential. Not only does it leave us feeling bad about ourselves, it also hinders our ability to make positive changes. Rewiring our brains to adopt positive affirmations takes effort, but anyone can do it, and it works. I suggest keeping a diary and writing down your thoughts during a difficult situation. Draw a line in the middle of the page. On one side, write your negative self-talk. On the other side, write a relatable, healthy affirmation. This process will help you become more conscious of your thoughts, enabling you to move forward with a more positive sense of self. Over time, these affirmations will become your new inner voice. For example:

- "I am the worst mom" becomes "I make mistakes, but that doesn't make me the worst mom."
- "My kids deserve better" becomes "I am enough."

The Pressure

Today the pressure of being a "successful" mother can leave us feeling inadequate and stressed. There's a big difference between thoughtfully educating yourself and giving in to inappropriate parenting ideals. In a world where social media declares what perfect parenting looks like, it's hard to prevent these ideals from influencing the decisions we make. The mother who does yoga with her child on her head. The father who plays football with the kids while mom rests. The adorable matching pajamas for the family on holiday nights. The mom who makes themed cookies (with no sugar) on Super Bowl Sunday. The beautiful family picture on the beach. Social media has a way of triggering our insecurities. Everyone is doing a better job at life than me! I have had countless phone calls from women who tell me that other moms or husbands "do" more. And it's true; some do. But I always say, "It's a package deal. Do you want to know what else is in the package?" Meaning, we are only seeing parts of the whole.

Take it from me; those images on social media are just glimpses of people's lives, not the entire picture. My mother likes to say, "If they have to show it to the world, there is something to hide." Perhaps that's true, but at the very least, we cannot assume a picture defines a person's or a family's entire life's story. And don't forget: there is no such thing as a perfect family. Keep your eyes on your own path, and remember that you are good enough as you are.

The Perfect Parent

We all have the same goal: to be the best parents we can be. We are constantly worried that our children will suffer because of our mistakes. We are consumed by our children's wellbeing. We want to get straight A's across the board! The funny thing is, there is no parenting grading system. It only exists in our minds, where it pulls at our insecurities. We need to adjust our expectations of ourselves. We aren't superheroes. There is no such thing as being a perfect parent. As I mentioned above, you need to keep telling yourself, "I am not perfect, but I am enough." If you are constantly striving to be perfect—whatever that means—you are not only setting yourself up for failure; more importantly, you are also setting your kids up for failure. You end up focusing on the pressure instead of the journey. In fact, accepting yourself even when you could have done a better job is a healthy lesson to model for your children. If you cannot accept yourself, you will never be able to accept your children for who they are. Acceptance means knowing your strengths *and* your weaknesses and then accepting both. You don't have to be perfect to accept yourself. Likewise, your children don't need to be perfect to feel accepted by you.

Self-Growth

All that being said, we do need to be open to growth. This process begins by ignoring the inner voice that says, "My child needs to listen to me" or "I am the parent" or "This child needs to change if he wants to be part of this family." I am referring here to the mindsets and beliefs we have inherited from generations past asserting that children belong to parents and owe them unconditional obedience. The more we succumb to this egotistic mindset, the less we will grow as a people *and* as parents.

Someone once told me, "If you want to know where you need to improve, look no further than your relationship with your kids." Kids have a way of highlighting the personal areas we need to improve in, such as stretching our patience, practicing self-control, or becoming more accepting. Since parenthood is closest to home for all mothers, both physically and emotionally, we will be surrounded by mirrors of self-growth during this stage of our lives. The tests of parenthood can stimulate growth if we allow them to do so. If we don't fight this process, we will come to recognize that we aren't the same person we were before we became parents. This process of selflessness inevitably leads to becoming our best selves.

Adjusting Expectations According to Your Children's Way

As a mother, I can tell you that from the moment you give birth, all you pray for is that your kids will be successful in every possible way: the star athlete, the doctor, the captain of the dance team, the social butterfly, the addiction-free child, the child who battles through tough times, the child who is respectful, responsible, and successful. However, as my kids began to grow up, I became very aware that my goals for them were not in their own best interests. Indeed, those goals were in *my* best interest.

When my oldest was two years old, I read every book under the sun to her. I wanted her to go to school and excel, to have a better experience than I did. I went above and beyond to make sure she was "up to par" (whatever that means).

17

I admit it was kind of nuts, and eventually, I had to take a step back. After some self-reflection, I understood that I was, in fact, dumping my own "baggage" onto her. I had an epiphany and developed a theory I call "Detached Parenting." It sounds neglectful but it's not. It's a mindset that says the following:

> My children are not a reflection of my past or present self. Their journeys are not for me to choose. Children are not here for us to live vicariously through, nor were they born to mirror our successes. I will not parent my children to fulfill my hopes and dreams because that will compromise who they are as individuals.

When we impose our expectations onto our children, we are essentially dumping our psychological and emotional baggage onto them. Whether we expect them to become successful in the ways that we are or live vicariously through them and hope they will become who we have struggled to be, we are suppressing our children's individuality. We need to see our children as separate beings who are not an extension of us.

Redefining Success

Once you take yourself out of the equation, we will see that your children's success will look different from how you've defined it for yourself. The New Oxford American dictionary defines success as "the accomplishment of an aim or purpose." Note that it does not define "success" as "smart, popular, athletic, artistic, creative, etc." "Success" is subjective; it differs for each person. For example, a child who has a learning disability will find success in being able to read fluently, whereas for another child, that will be routine. Your job as a parent is to define success according to each child's characteristics and unique needs, assist them on their journey, and then watch them blossom as individuals. Allowing your children to walk their own path is the greatest gift you can give them.

Children will likely struggle to feel successful if they compare themselves or their achievements to others. Likewise, if you compare your children to others, you will hinder their growth. For example, my oldest daughter, Vivian, is bright and intuitive and has a passion for understanding how people work. (I don't know where she gets that from!) My other daughter, Frieda, my second child, is super creative, marches to her own beat, dances the day away, and loves art. If my husband and

I defined success by a one-size-fits-all "ideal," our girls would grow up feeling insecure and unhappy. They would go through life competing for positions that aren't in line with their personalities. It is thus imperative to define "success" by allowing our unconditional acceptance to guide our vision of what that looks like for each child.

To help me stay on course with each of my children, I have written a mission statement that we follow for each child. Whenever my husband and I are having trouble making a decision, we go back to that child's mission statement and ask ourselves, "Does taking this approach align with this child's mission statement?" The decision then becomes clearer for us. Here are two examples of our mission statements.

- "Our mission is to guide our daughter on a path of success by keeping in mind her consistency to follow through, her determination to succeed, and her strong will to make the world a better place. We will do our part by assisting her in ways that are consistent with her strengths and values. We will give her the independence she needs, and we will redirect her when she is not being true to herself. We will continue to nourish her mind and soul by providing opportunities to explore her passions. We will instill the beauty of our faith, our family values, and our traditions."
- "Our mission is to guide our son on a path of success by providing him with the patience that he needs and the proper resources to succeed. We will provide an environment for him to exert his energy and share in his interest of movement and activity. We will pave the way for future success by providing exposure in areas that will cultivate his beautiful character and abundance of energy. We will instill the importance of faith, our values, and our traditions, and we will hold his hand through life with unconditional love."

The Importance of Just Being

So often as parents we lose precious opportunities to just be with our children because we are so focused on parenting the "right" way and ensuring their success. Parenting mindfully is important, but the essence of parenting lies in authentic connection. Being fully present in the moments you spend with your children means you aren't focusing on what you *should* be doing or what lesson you *could* be teaching but simply enjoying your time with them.

"But Norma," you may be thinking, "how do we connect with our children when we are so focused on parenting with the right approach? Doesn't mindful parenting require us to be somewhat calculated and scripted? How can we be present with our kids and meaningfully connect with them if we are constantly in our heads?"

I have an analogy for this great question. Imagine you are a successful actor on Broadway. You've practiced your part for months. You know the script through and through. But when the time comes to perform, you let all that go and actually live the part. The same goes for parenting. Prep, prep, and prep. But when you are connecting with your children, you need to move all that you've learned to the back of your mind and allow yourself to be in the moment. In other words, throw the script out the window, and just be with your kids. Here lies the balance between parenting mindfully and authentically connecting with your children.

For example, one day my daughter was recounting her day at school. She told me about a boy blowing bubbles with his gum and how the teacher kept telling him to spit it out. She said the boy kept blowing bubbles while the class was cracking up. I bit my tongue because I wanted to teach her that gum chewing and acting disrespectful to the teacher was inappropriate. However, my daughter was simply chitchatting with me about her funny experience. Luckily, I stopped myself and just laughed along with her. I redirected my focus and embraced the chance to connect with her.

Over the years I have come to learn that there are plenty of opportunities to teach children, but we must also allow time simply to enjoy being together. Human beings are always evolving, and being present is a state of mind, not a destination. Just as we evolve, so do our children, and meeting them where they are with an open mind and a willingness to support them each day allows us to be present in each and every moment as it comes.

No handbook can tell you exactly how to parent your child (except this one—just kidding!). Parenting books and classes are great tools for educating yourself, and learning different parenting approaches can be helpful, but there are some things you can only learn from your children. Children tell us what they need if we take the time to be present and listen. Once you see them and hear them, you will feel empowered to provide opportunities for them to blossom. Given that I've read every parenting book under the sun and listened to countless parenting classes, I can say with certainty that if you are authentically connected to your children, you are the only one who will know what is truly best for them. Remember, there is no single template for parenting. Trust your intuition when filtering out what works for you and your family.

The Takeaway

Although reflecting on your past can teach you a lot about how you arrived at your current parenting approach, the challenge—and opportunity—is learning how to parent with consciousness and intent. Gaining insight into your present self by understanding the past provides stepping stones into your future role as a parent committed to unconditional love and acceptance. Then you can move forward on your parenting journey with self-acceptance, trust in your innate intuition, and the knowledge that you are the best fit for your children.

Quotes to Hold On To

"Knowing yourself is the beginning of all wisdom."
—Aristotle (philosopher)

"Our children can be our greatest teachers if we are humble enough to receive their lessons."
—Bryan McGill (bestselling author, activist, and social entrepreneur)

"Your child may need a different parenting style than what you needed growing up. Parent the child you have, not the child you were."
—Dr. Jenn Hardy (psychologist and author)

2

The Orchestra

Imagine you are watching an orchestra. On the raised podium stands the conductor. He is responsible for directing the performance by understanding the music and conveying it through gestures to the musicians. His role allows the musicians to perform a unified vision of the music and create a symphony. The importance of the conductor's role is critical. While an orchestra may consist of very talented musicians, their performance will inevitably fall short without a skillful conductor. Each musician plays a key role in the performance; each has his own talent, her own gift. The conductor skillfully highlights their talents and strengths while drawing out their excellence. With the conductor's direction and intuition, the orchestra plays in unison and harmony, and the symphony flows beautifully and naturally.

Now imagine that a conductor cues the wrong musician at the wrong time or doesn't direct the piece at the proper speed. As a result, the music becomes incoherent and chaotic. Imagine that the conductor does not recognize the musicians' individual talents or that he favors one of the musicians over others and assigns this musician the largest solo. The other members of the orchestra will likely become frustrated, angry, and insecure in their positions. The orchestra will struggle to perform in harmony, and once again, the symphony risks being ruined.

The Process

As a parent, you are a conductor, and your family is your orchestra. Each of your children has a unique gift, a spark that needs care and support in order to ignite their potential. With the most delicate gesture, you can help your children recognize what makes them special. When children are aware of their special qualities, they know their position in the family and what they bring to the table. Most importantly, they are content in themselves. They begin to form a healthy foundation of self-esteem. When children know that they—and only they—can illuminate the world with their unique spark, they will not rely on their ego or false sense of self while navigating the world. They will feel secure and less likely to act out, and your home will flow naturally and harmoniously.

In my thirteen years of attaining a PhD in motherhood, I have discovered a four-step process for helping children develop healthy self-esteem.

Step 1: Highlight your Child's Goodness

The first step in helping your children develop healthy self-esteem is to recognize and highlight their uniqueness, or what I refer to as their "spark."

A spark is a light that shines from within. It is a natural goodness that your child brings to the world. As children grow up, it becomes easier to see the goodness they gravitate toward. Are they kindhearted? Do they like to give to others? Do they hurt for a friend who is hurting? Do they make people laugh? These are all examples of little sparks that need care and support, so your kids can cultivate and explore the unique strengths and gifts they bring to the world.

It's important to note that a spark is never something physical, such as being beautiful or a great athlete. I call these "surface accomplishments."

- "You are the most beautiful girl in the world."
- "You are the best swimmer."
- "You are the next Michael Jordan!"
- "You have the biggest muscles."
- "You are the fastest rider."

Superficial compliments are empty and unreliable. Complimenting your children on physical qualities and accomplishments sends the message that, "You are valuable if you are beautiful." "You are successful if you are the best athlete." However, when children are faced with a more beautiful person or a better swimmer, they say to themselves, "If I'm not the best, then what am I worth? What do I have to offer?"

We are more than just physical beings; our spiritual and emotional selves need to be cultivated. If you over-emphasize your children's physical accomplishments or genes and don't focus on their inner qualities, you will suppress their ability to create a life filled with meaning and purpose—the core of true self-esteem.

When celebrity basketball player Kobe Bryant passed away in a helicopter crash in early 2020, the world was devastated by his loss, and everyone was grieving. While watching the news reports, I learned an important lesson. People were not eulogizing him by talking about his basketball career, his talents off the court, or his net worth. They were remembering him for his devotion as a father, husband, friend, and leader. Some of his most beautiful and motivational statements on and off the court were quoted all over the Internet. I have yet to learn how many NBA titles he won, how many points he scored, or how much money he was worth. Although most people know this information, no one cares because it's not important. Ironically, the day before his passing, Bryant tweeted support for his pal Lebron James for surpassing his own NBA all-time scoring record. It is obvious to me that Bryant did not rely on his basketball career to feel successful. Instead, he used his platform to fulfill his purpose by spreading love and inspiring people to work hard and persevere in the face of difficulty. His positive influence on the world surpassed his numbers on the scoreboard or the balance of his bank account.

Step 2: Position Your Children to Match Their Strengths

After you recognize and highlight your children's goodness, the second step is to take a hard look at their personalities, so you can provide the right opportunities for their spark to ignite. Making the connection between their personalities and their goodness is how you can begin to connect the dots in providing your kids with opportunities to feel and be successful. Luckily, we are all born with personalities that are tailor-made for our purpose. Every person enters this world with a unique set of personality "cards" that makes them who they are. The way we play our cards determines how we impact the world. Our cards were given to us intentionally, knowing this is the best deck of cards to achieve individual greatness. That is why you should not try to change your children's personalities. It is much better to direct them in a way that catalyzes their unique strengths and personalities.

Step 3: Provide Opportunities for Success

The third step is to place your children in positions or situations where they can feel and be successful. For example, if a child is strong willed and determined, give them tasks that allow them to explore leadership roles. Likewise, if a child is shy, don't put them in a position where they're forced to speak in public. Instead, recognize the value of being quiet and reflective, and highlight those strengths. Assigning the same tasks to different children who demonstrate different strengths can lead to jealousy, sibling rivalry, and poor self-esteem. Understanding your children's personality strengths and providing opportunities for them to build on those will not only contribute to healthy self-esteem but will also harness those attributes for a life full of meaning and purpose.

Here are some examples of the first three steps of the process.

- "Grandma had a hard day today. You always have the perfect words for people who are hurting. I know you're busy, but I feel you are the best person for the job if you'd like to call her."
- "Daddy isn't feeling well, and you are a very caring person. Do you want to see if he needs some Advil or tea?"
- "It's Uncle Jackie's birthday today. I could use a funny joke to write him in the card. You always make people laugh! Can you help me?"
- "Ronnie is almost two, and he's afraid to walk to the store with Mommy! You have a gentle touch with him, and he trusts you. Would you be able to hold his hand? "
- "Doing homework with your sister is difficult for me when the baby needs a bottle. I notice you have a lot of patience with your sister. Do you think you can help her tonight?"

Whether your child is determined and strong minded, shy and sensitive, creative, or free willed, it is your job as the conductor to orchestrate their personalities so they can feel successful by knowing their unique roles. This will allow your home to flow naturally and harmoniously.

Here are some examples of how to use these steps with different personality types.

The bossy, determined, strong-willed child. This is the kid who needs to win the family game of Monopoly, who doesn't want to wait his or her turn, who runs to their room when his or her playdate won't follow her rules.

- Ask for the child's help in organizing a family activity. For example, "Honey, Daddy and I want to dedicate a day to giving back to the community, but we're having trouble coming up with ideas. I think you would be the perfect person to organize this day for our family. You're a hard worker and have a knack for choosing the right roles for people so that everything goes smoothly. Are you up for the task?"

- Assign your child the job of dinner menu organizer. Have him or her ask family members for ideas and then design a menu for the week that satisfies everyone. For example, "Jackie, you are my right-hand man in this family. You are responsible, efficient, and extremely helpful. I am having trouble accommodating everyone's dinner requests, and I could really use your help in organizing the dinner menu for the upcoming week. I know that you are both considerate and fair and will try your best to accommodate everyone's requests. Are you up for the task?"

- Ask your child to research ideas for possible family trips. For example, "Rebecca, Daddy and I would like to plan a family vacation. I could use your help in coming up with ideas and all the planning. I know you have a busy week ahead of you, but you are the best person for this job! Can you find the time to help me?"

The creative, free-spirited child. This is the child who TikToks all day, who dresses in a tutu for school, and who draws a smiley on your couch.

- Ask the child to help plan fun family events. For example, "Honey, I could use your help in coming up with a theme for daddy's birthday. I want to throw a surprise party that shows him how much he means to us, and you have a way of using your creativity in a very personal and beautiful way."

- Ask your child to help design the sign for the lemonade stand his or her sibling is hosting to help raise money for school. For example, "Sharon, your siblings are raising money for a beautiful cause that will help needy families. You are the perfect person to design the sign for the lemonade stand. I know your siblings can really use your help. Your role is really important to this project because it will help attract people to stop by and donate."

- Assign your child the job of decorating the house during the holidays. For example, "Michael, the holidays are coming up. I want to make our home really festive, and I could use your help in

27

ideas for decorating. I know I can probably manage on my own, but with your help, I know that it will turn out great and the holidays will be more special for everyone."

The goofy child. This is the child who burps at the dinner table, who mimics you when you're angry, who keeps tapping on your leg after you told them not to more than once.

- Ask the child to help lighten the mood. For example, "Your brother is having a tough day, and you always know how to make everyone around you happy. Can you stay up an extra ten minutes to hang out with him?"
- Invite your child to host a karaoke night for the family. For example, "Sarah, Daddy and I feel we need a fun family night, so we decided on organizing a karaoke night this Thursday. You are the perfect person for the job to host it. With your upbeat and hilarious personality, the night will be entertaining for everyone."
- Ask your child to come up with some funny costume ideas for the family for the holidays. For example, "David, Purim is coming up. We need some family costume ideas. I need your help in coming up with a theme for us. We need to come up with some costume ideas. You are the perfect person to set the tone for the holiday. With your help, I know that our family will really stand out and really enjoy the holiday."
- Assign your child the job of writing a poem with personal jokes of Grandpa for his sixtieth birthday party. For example, "Esther, Grandpa's sixtieth birthday party is coming up. Who better to help me write his birthday poem than you? I need you and all your funny jokes to make it really special for him."

The all-over-the-place child. This is the child you are always chasing out the door to catch the school bus, who splashes everyone in the pool, and whose teacher is on speed dial.

- Enroll their help in high-energy activities. For example, "Honey, you have the most energy in this house. I need your help in collecting money for this big fundraiser. It's going to be exhausting for me, but if anyone can do it, it's you!"
- Assign your child the role of being "lifeguard" at the pool for the day to emphasize the importance of following the rules at the pool. For example, "Eddie, we are hosting a lot of people by our house today. There are going to be ten children by the pool. Daddy suggested we hire a lifeguard, but then we remembered

that we have you! You are responsible and have the energy to run around and keep a watch on all the kids. I need your help in making sure everyone follows the safety rules of the pool. Would you be able to assist me today?"

- Ask your child to create a scavenger hunt or obstacle course for guests who are coming over. For example, "Betty, we are having a couple of families over for the day tomorrow. I want the kids to feel comfortable and be entertained. I was thinking about organizing a scavenger hunt for them. I can use your help in planning it and helping the kids through it. You always know how to stay active and have a good time. Can you help me?"

- Ask your child's teacher to allow him to be the teacher's helper for the day. For example, "Mrs. Cohen, as you know, Noah can use some help in staying engaged throughout the day. At home, I noticed that when Noah is "my helper" and feels "in charge," he really stays on task and beams with confidence. Would you be able to try taking this approach in school? Thank you for all your efforts."

- Give your child the "special mission" of running to grandma's house to surprise her with flowers. For example, "Joyce, I have a special mission that only you can do. We need to surprise Grandma with flowers, and she will be home in an hour. You are the perfect person for this mission. Are you up for the task?"

Once your children understand their position in the family, they will not compete for other's roles. They will see only their own path, a path full of purpose and meaning. This is more beautiful than any symphony.

Step 4: Drive Their Role Home

OK, so your daughter organized the dinner menu for the week, and your son delivered flowers to Grandma. You have provided opportunities for your children to feel successful, and you've praised their efforts. There is one more step to raise their self-esteem to even greater heights: expand on your children's accomplishments by showing them how their actions impacted the bigger picture. For example:

- "Jane, thank you for organizing the dinner menu this week. It helped my week run smoothly and efficiently. But do you know what else you did? Because of you, I was able to have some much needed 'mommy time' and go for lunch with some friends today. I came home happier and calmer. Not only did you free up some time for me, your act of kindness also contributed to the well-being of the whole family. Thank you."

- "Albert, delivering flowers to Grandma is such a special act of kindness. I imagine Grandma walking down the stairs tomorrow and smiling. But you should know that it's not only the beautiful flowers that will make Grandma smile this week; it's the message that comes with them. The beautiful flowers that you delivered show Grandma that she has people who love and care for her, and that message will stay with her long after the flowers are gone."
- "Honey, when you helped your sister up after she fell down, I noticed the other children at the park were watching. Not only did you show your sister such kindness, you also showed the other children what it looks like to help someone when they fall. Maybe those children will follow your example. People like you make the world a better place."

Broadening your children's perspective on the importance of their roles empowers them. It reinforces the idea that their spark is not confined to a moment or their inner circle but can illuminate the entire world.

Remind Me Again Why Self-Esteem Is so Important

When it comes to parenting, self-esteem is a hot topic; it's almost impossible to find a parenting book that doesn't address it. But what's the big deal? What can children gain by having healthy self-esteem? Quite a few things, actually. Self-esteem can help your children:

- Make healthy choices
- Take healthy risks
- Realize their self-worth
- Follow through when tasks become difficult to achieve
- Cope with disappointing situations
- Resist negative social influences
- Feel secure in who they are and what they stand for
- Be more resilient

To illustrate, here are some examples of statements from children with low self-esteem.

- "I'm going to lose."
- "I'm not playing anymore."
- "I won't join the lesson because I'm not good at it."
- "I'm stupid."
- "I'm never going to do well."

- "Why bother?"
- "My friends think I'm an idiot."

Now, here are some examples of statements from children who have healthy self-esteem.

- "Although I failed this test, if I try harder, I know I can do better."
- "I'm not going to this party. I know it's not going to be my scene, and it may put me in an uncomfortable situation."
- "I'm nervous about basketball tryouts, but whether I make the team or not, I'll enjoy the experience and continue to play."
- "I know I am hurting right now, but I will come out of this stronger."
- "I don't smoke. I do not care what you think."
- "I don't have all the answers, but that is perfectly OK."

I heard a lecture in which the speaker compared self-esteem to poker chips. Kids with high self-esteem have lots of chips. They are willing to take chances and know their worth. Children with low self-esteem have fewer chips. When they say, "I don't want to go to school today," they are really saying, "I don't have enough chips to get in the game." Some children with few chips play with them recklessly. They say, "I guess I'll bet the whole thing. I don't care." Such children make bad choices, like joining a gang or taking drugs. Other children with few chips are conservative. They may say, "No, I don't want to make anything for the science fair." What they are really saying is, "I'm going to hold on to the few chips I have. I can't risk losing them."

After explaining his concept of chips, the speaker posed the question: "What if your child doesn't have enough poker chips?" His answer: "Give them chips." Find the one thing that child is good at, and make it a big deal. Celebrate it. If a child is good at using a screwdriver, loosen every screw in the house and say, "I need you. Nobody does it like you."

Our experiences in this world affect our self-esteem. If a child is a strong student, athletic, charming, good looking, and popular, he or she will likely have better experiences and more poker chips to play with. But self-esteem can't be based solely on external measures of success. Superficial accomplishments that do not hold inherent meaning and purpose may contribute to a child's self-esteem, but they won't deliver a deeper sense of value. You need to focus on fostering *innate* abilities and satisfaction.

Self-esteem is about valuing yourself. It is about knowing who you are and accepting yourself unconditionally—the good, the bad, and the ugly. It allows for positive relationships, love, success, growth, tolerance, and peace. When you give your kids the gift of self-esteem, it will keep giving for the rest of their lives.

Quotes to Hold On To

"The child must know that he is a miracle, that since the beginning of the world there has not been, and until the end of the world there will not be, another child like him."
—Pau Casals (Catalan composer and conductor thought to be one of the greatest cellists of all time)

"Behind every child who believes in himself is a parent who believed first."
—Matthew L. Jacobson

"No act of kindness is too small. The gift of kindness may start as a small ripple that over time can turn into a tidal wave affecting the lives of many."
—Kevin Heath

3

Unconditional

Remember the feeling you had when your baby was born? That overwhelming sense of unconditional love and acceptance? Over time and for various reasons, we lose that sense of pure, unconditional acceptance. Maybe it's because infants are so vulnerable and don't talk back to us. Perhaps it's because they don't push our buttons like a five-year-old or a teenager. Whatever the reasons, you need to remind yourself that the blessing is still there. The same child is right in front of you with the same emotional needs as that little baby. We can get so caught up in the emotional roller-coaster ride of parenting that sometimes we need to find our way back to that original place of gratitude and love without the if's, ands, or buts.

Loving your children unconditionally means accepting them as is for exactly who they are. You can do that through your responses to your children's behavior—your voice, your tone, and your body language—when your kids make mistakes. If you want to fix or change your children, they will sense it—and they will resist it. If you love them only when they are "good," you are sending the message of *conditional* love. Conditional love means your love must be earned. It's like saying, "If you act the way we want you to, we will love you." Conditional love is a form of control: "Conform to meet my needs, or I will not love or accept you." This is not love; it is approval. Your children will always strive to get that love and attention. If you raise your kids to earn your love, they will carry that emotional baggage into adulthood. Love should never be dependent on behavior. Love is unconditional by definition.

What Does Acceptance Look Like?

We all want to feel accepted just as we are. Acceptance is the polar opposite of conditional love. It is unconditional, the ultimate form of love. When parents accept their children, they lay the groundwork for their children to accept themselves. What does unconditional love and acceptance look like? Here are some examples.
- I accept that my child can be stubborn.
- I accept that my child has a lot of energy.
- I accept that my child is shy.
- I accept that my child is messy.
- I accept that my child can be arrogant.
- I accept that my child is fearful.
- I accept that my child is selfish.
- I accept that my child is sensitive.
- I accept that my child has ADHD.
- I accept that my child is impulsive.
- I accept that my child does not like sports.
- I accept that my child does not share my interests.
- I accept my child for exactly who he or she is—as is.

Once you accept your children, you can reframe the way you perceive their character traits. Every trait can be judged as being positive or negative. When you are able to see the positive in *every* character trait, you can cultivate them. If you perceive any traits as negative, you will limit their ability to be an asset for your children in their future. Remember: children will sense whether you are trying to fix or mold them. If your children come to define certain character traits as negative because of messages you've communicated, you will hinder their growth and potential. Here are some examples of reframing negative character traits into positive ones.
- Stubborn → Persistent

- Wild → Energetic
- Strong-minded → Determined
- Shy → Modest
- Messy → Creative
- Arrogant → Confident
- Fearful → Cautious
- Selfish → Self-aware of his or her needs
- Sensitive → Empathetic
- ADHD → Multitasker and Energetic
- Impulsive → Risk-taker

The Difference Between Cultivating and "Fixing" Character Traits

How you work with your child's temperament depends on your perception of your child's character traits and your intentions. Cultivating a character trait means building on a trait that already exists—expanding and developing what is. Fixing a child's traits means trying to change them. In thinking about this difference, the first question to ask yourself is, *Do I want to fix my child to make him or her easier to handle, or am I concerned with how best to support the child?*

Freeing yourself from the mindset that your kids need to be "fixed" can be liberating. Children will never act perfectly. They are going to make mistakes and bad choices. It is how you respond to those imperfections that can make or break the child. The way you talk to your children becomes their inner voice. Children carry their parents' voice on their journey throughout life. It's the voice they hear when facing difficulties, failure, and important decisions. Is the voice kind and patient, loving and accepting? Or is it filled with criticism and self-doubt? Again, the way you talk to your children will become the way they talk to themselves. Make sure it's a comforting voice.

Of course, we still love our kids even when we disapprove of their behavior, but children aren't always able to differentiate between love and approval. To be clear, unconditional love does *not* mean you approve of all your children's behavior. It means you approve of your children regardless of their behavior. You can communicate your love while also communicating disapproval by separating the child from his or her misbehavior. It's the difference between "You always hit your brother" and "It is unacceptable to use our hands for hitting in this house." The first message shows disapproval of the child that is tied to disapproval of his or her behavior. The second message implies acceptance of the child while disapproving of the child's behavior.

Although it can be overwhelming to realize the impact you have on your children's lives, it can also empower you to grow. That is the beauty of life; it is never too late for growth. Growth is not a destination; it's a journey.

Quotes to Hold On To

"The beginning of love is to let those we love be perfectly themselves, and not to twist them to fit our own image. Otherwise, we love only the reflection of ourselves we find in them."
—Thomas Merton

"The greatest gift you can give to others is the gift of unconditional love and acceptance."
—Brian Tracy

"Children don't just need to know they are loved; they need to know that nothing they do will change the fact that they are loved."
—Alfie Kohn (American author and lecturer)

PART II: THE HOME

4

The United Front

At some point on the journey, most couples will differ on how to approach parenting. If your home is like many, the next few examples may sound familiar.

> Mom: "Charles, it's time for bed!"
> Child: "But I'm in the middle of watching my show!"
> Dad: "Honey, let him finish the show. There's only twenty minutes left."

> Dad: "You can't speak like that to me. I'm your father!"
> Mom: "He's just tired and cranky. You need to leave him alone when he's in a mood."
> Child: "Yeah! Mommy's right!"

> Child: "Can I go to Steven's house to watch the game?"
> Mom: "No, honey, tonight is not a good night."

Dad: "Why can't he go? His friends are all there?"

Presenting a united front when it comes to parenting will enable you to discipline your children effectively and, more importantly, allows for a peaceful home filled with love, respect, and consistency.

"That's beautiful, Norma," you may say, "but realistically, is united parenting possible when two parents don't share the same views?"

Yes. In fact, different views on parenting can actually be helpful when it comes to raising children. You and your partner don't have to agree on every issue that comes up. Rather, the importance lies in how you handle those differences and learn from them. The goal is to appreciate the value in both sets of ideas and then co-create a parenting approach that is right for your children.

Getting on the Same Page

Before thinking about how to parent on the same page as your partner, you must first do some good ol' self-reflecting by asking yourself the following:

- How do my partner and I usually address our differences? Do we argue with each other in front of our children?
- Do we undermine each other when faced with disagreements?
- Do we show respect for each other even when we disagree?
- Do we ask for support when it comes to a decision one of us has made but disregard each other's opinions when asking for input?
- Do we show support for each other no matter what?
- Do we model healthy disagreements?

Remember: modeling is your strongest tool when it comes to showing respect, communicating honestly, and accepting disagreements. This conduct will speak louder than the topic being addressed.

Even for parents who are typically on the same page, it's impossible to agree on every issue that comes up. For example, if parents disagree on how to discipline a child for a particular misbehavior, it's best to discuss the situation without the child present: "Daddy and I would like a few minutes to discuss this in our room."

Some parents truly do have fundamental differences in how children should be raised. One parent may feel the other is too strict and that there are too many rules to follow. Or a parent may feel that their partner isn't invested enough and simply wants to avoid conflict. Another common disagreement is when a parent has a "soft spot" for a specific child and avoids disciplining that child. Parenting can often highlight our differences, and for many couples, it can really put a strain on the marriage. When parents disagree and can't resolve their differences, it creates a dynamic that children take advantage of to avoid consequences.

Although challenging, such marital disagreements aren't uncommon, and for a lot of parents, parenting can actually bring them closer together.

The process of united parenting begins by communicating with your partner about your commitment to the relationship and your desire to create a shared vision for your children and how to parent them. If you approach your "other" and only address the topic of parenting, he or she is likely to get defensive. When you preface it by expressing a desire and commitment to unite, it lays the foundation for an open conversation. Then you discuss your children's goals, personalities, and strengths and where some improvement might be needed. It can be especially helpful to create a mission statement for each child that addresses how to best support them as individuals (see chapter 2 for more on creating mission statements.) When you're having difficulty making decisions, a mission statement can provide the clarity you need by giving you a goal to work toward. Once you have a mission statement, you can discuss which parenting approach will help get your child there. You will inevitably find common ground in certain areas and differences in other areas. The question to ask yourself is, "What approach should we take to help meet each child's needs?"

The goal is to come together, listen to your partner, learn from each other, value your partner's opinion, and be open to criticism. If your partner feels there are too many rules in the house, be open to prioritizing. If your partner is not invested enough, share your concerns and how much you need your partner to be engaged. If you feel your partner avoids disciplining out of fear of hurting the child, discuss the effects of parenting without discipline. Express a commitment to making more of an effort to meeting your partner's needs and, more importantly, your commitment to building your relationship. Highlight the importance of parenting on the same page, not only for the kids' sake but as a way to support each other on your parenting journey. Remember, just like parenting, a healthy marriage takes work.

Navigating Differences

Although united parenting is the goal, certain areas of parenting can be more difficult or even impossible to compromise on—decisions having to do with religious and spiritual orientation, managing health issues, which schools to choose, and balancing home and work life, among others. Parents often tell me that when it was just the two of them, those differences never really came up. But after a child was added to the mix, those differences smacked them in the face. Children have a way of doing that.

For many couples, much of the conflict around parenting stems from issues in their relationship. Parents sometimes express their dissatisfaction with each other by disapproving of each other's parenting practices. Even when partners have the best intentions in regard to parenting, addressing problems in their marriage may be necessary before they can parent collaboratively. It's surprising how many parents don't connect healthy parenting with a healthy marriage. Yes, you can be a good parent even during struggles with your partner, but a happy, healthy marriage directly affects and contributes to your children's well-being.

Unfortunately, parenting with a united front is simply unattainable for many people because a strained marriage will not allow for it, especially in the case of divorce. There is only so much in life we can control, and we just have to do the best we can with the cards we are dealt. However, whenever possible, parents should try to find a middle ground and put aside their differences, so they can focus on their children's needs. At the very least, a parent's love and connection will go a long way, even when they stand on their own.

Lastly but most important, never compromise with your partner when it comes to a child's emotional wellbeing. If a parent hurts, embarrasses, or speaks in a detrimental tone to his or her child, there is no room for compromise. It is simply unacceptable. That parent needs to be gently told that their behavior is not OK. If they keep struggling to parent in a healthy way, that parent should seek professional help.

Although challenging at times, parenting with a united voice allows for a peaceful home and more secure children. A peaceful home provides nurturing and warmth. Children are sponges. They pick up on everything. When a home is full of tension with two opposing voices, children will be affected, even if it's not intentional. They may respond in ways you do not understand or notice, but they will respond.

As the title of this book says, "I am not a psychologist." While I would love to be able to guide couples through their difficulties, it is not within my domain. My advice would be to explore your differences with an open mind. If you need help navigating the conversation, find a good psychologist, therapist, or counselor. A commitment to your partner and your family is always worth the investment. Parents who strive to make their home a loving and peaceful environment, full of respect and mutual support, are laying the foundation for their children to become loving, nurturing adults.

Quotes to Hold On To

"Coming together is a beginning; keeping together is a process; working together is success."
—Henry Ford (American Industrialist, founder of the Ford Motor company)

—Edward Everett Hale (American author, poet, and historian)
"A great marriage is not when the 'perfect couple' comes together. It is when an imperfect couple learns to enjoy their differences."

—David Meurer (Award-winning author and writer)
"The best security blanket a child can have is parents who respect each other."
—Jane Blaustone

5

Discipline

B ack when I was a kid, when we were "bad," we were punished. We never really knew what the punishment would be, but we were afraid of it. Historically, discipline has been a one-size-fits-all affair, doled out quickly, efficiently, and maybe even roughly. At school if a child was fidgeting at his desk, he was punished. No parent/teacher-school psychologist-principal meeting was set up, and there was certainly no recommendation for an evaluation or a customized response. A child with ADHD who misbehaved during class—who only had twenty minutes of run-around time during recess to burn his energy—was punished by having to work at their desk during recess. Lesson learned. The child didn't fidget at his desk anymore.

During one of his stand-up routines, comedian Sebastian Maniscalco tells a story about sitting in a restaurant with his wife's family. His wife's nephew disappeared from the table, came in from behind him, and "chopped" him in the back of his neck with his hand. The kid's parents looked up and said, "Oh well, he's just a kid." Maniscalco referred back to his upbringing and said, "Do you know what would happen to me if I slapped an adult at a restaurant? Right? My father would come from behind me, put a black bag over my head, and take me to an undisclosed location. I would return one hour later, a brand-new kid. There would be a lot of bowing: 'I am so sorry. I am so sorry. My father just informed me that I will be working for you for the next twelve years of my life.'" It's the funniest skit I have ever seen, and it's true. Many adults in my generation say, "But we grew up fine!" My response is, "I want to meet you, and I doubt it!" Even if we did grow up "fine," it's because we grew up in a different time in a different world with different expectations and norms.

Fast-forward to today, and the gap between the parent/child role has tightened. More than ever before, parents know about child development and strive to meet their children's emotional needs. We search the Internet for parenting advice, read books about parenting, attend parenting classes, and seek help and support from friends, family members, and even professionals when needed. My mother jokes that my father never changed a diaper when we were growing up, and she laughs at how dads are so involved in childcare these days. My father claims we were all easy babies, and my mother always has the same answer: "What house were you living in?" All four of us were colicky, never slept through the night, and had apple juice bottles in our cribs. My mother was a walking zombie until we were all in school.

Growing up, my parents did not have many house rules, but my mother was firm on one: we weren't allowed to be "moody." If we crossed that line, we were put in our rooms until the mood disappeared. Today, if a child has a mood, we tread lightly and read up on how to deal with it. It's hard not to laugh at the ends we will go to, but the truth is, we are parenting according to *our* generation's norms, whether we like it or not.

My parenting approach is somewhere in between. I believe children need to be taught respect and be clear on the fact that we are not their friends but their parents. I also believe that instilling fear in children for "bad behavior" is not an effective long-term strategy. Kids will simply become smarter in the ways of sneaking around you. More importantly, you'll lose the privilege of teaching them. The process of raising children in this generation means building a relationship with them by addressing their emotional needs and disciplining when necessary *for the purpose of teaching*.

So, before discussing the topic of discipline, we need to consider *why* children misbehave. Here are some reasons I've discovered.

- They lack an emotional connection with their parents.

- They want attention.
- They are "living up" to the labels their parents identify them with.
- They want more independence and/or power and control.
- They lack skills of effective communication.
- They struggle to regulate their emotions.
- They aren't clear on the rules.
- Misbehavior helps them get what they want.
- They are human.

The next three sections of this admittedly long but important chapter attempt to address the vast topic of discipline.

I. THE VITAMINS

From the moment our children are born, we are attuned to their every physical need. We feed them every two hours, change their diapers just as often, and make sure they are up to date on their "wellness checks." As our babies grow up, they become less physically dependent and more emotionally dependent on us. As parents, we don't often adapt to this shift so quickly. We tend to keep focusing on their daily schedules and behavior. As a result, children's emotional needs can sometimes get overlooked, which is reflected in their behavior. They act out because those needs are not being met. At times they may feel disconnected, detached, unimportant, and maybe even "a burden." That's why it is so important to evaluate your relationship with your children and work toward building an even stronger one.

I like to refer to these strategies as "vitamins." If children get their daily dose, they can avoid getting sick or acting out in the first place. Here are the vitamins (with no particular association to specific strategies) to include in your everyday routine.

Vitamin C: Connecting with Your Children

Building a relationship with your kids is the foundation of parenting. There can be no discipline without a solid, meaningful relationship. Think about it: would you take advice from someone you aren't close to? Wouldn't you become defensive and point your finger back at them? Your connection to your children is the most powerful tool in the parenting toolbox. Other tools will come and go, but connection is the only tool that will be a constant on your parenting journey.

What is the process for building a strong bond with your kids? For small children, it can be as simple as play time and cuddles. For older children, it becomes a little more involved. Below are some strategies for building a connection with your children:

Time. The cornerstone of connecting with your children is spending time with them. It can be just listening to music, watching a TV show, dancing (while they make fun of you, of course), taking a walk, or building the Lego set that has been sitting in the closet since the holidays. It doesn't have to be a "great adventure." When I connect with my kids, I like to spend time with them in *their* territory, because it's where they feel more comfortable. If they are in their room listening to music, I plop onto the bed beside them. If they are watching TV, I bring them a snack and sit next to them. If they are outside shooting hoops, I join in. I don't make it a big deal; I just go with their flow and follow their lead.

Many people ask me how much time they should spend with their kids. I always say, "It's about quality, not quantity." It also depends on how much time they have available. If you have a child who is consistently misbehaving, focus on spending *more* time with that child. However you approach it, time spent with your children is a good investment (though you may not see an immediate return). Children need to know they are important to their parents. They need to know they are valuable and enjoyable to be around. Spending quality time with them will contribute to their self-esteem and overall well-being.

Positive non-verbal communication. From infancy through adulthood, a parent's nonverbal communication speaks volumes. The smile on your face, the glow in your eye contact, the hugs, cuddles, and kisses, and the way you look at your kids from afar. Do they see love and pride in your eyes? These simple, nonverbal gestures can speak louder than words and set the right stage when verbal communication begins.

For older children who have outgrown nursery rhymes and cuddles, keeping an open dialogue is a must if you want to connect with them. When your children come to you to talk or complain, the best way to connect is to validate their feelings—which includes nonverbal validation through your expressions, body language, and listening skills. Just being present in the moment and allowing your children to sit with their feelings is often enough to show you care for them and support them.

Verbal validation. You can also use your words to show your children that you understand their feelings, paving the way for open communication. To do so, you need to step into their shoes and feel what they are experiencing. Here are some examples of validating your children's feelings with your words.

- Child: "I am never going back to Jason's house."

- **Ineffective response** (a response that closes the door of open communication): "Why? What happened? He's so nice! I love his mom."
  - **Validating response:** "Oh man! You are so upset. Looks like you had a terrible time at his house."
- Child: "I am never going to school again."
  - **Ineffective response:** "Oh yes you are! You know the rule about missing school" or "If you did your homework, you wouldn't get in trouble."
  - **Validating response:** "Oh honey, I'm so sorry you had a bad day at school."
- Child: "Why did you make this dinner tonight? You know I hate it. You always make the worst dinners."
  - **Ineffective response:** "Are you joking? You're lucky you have a mom who makes you dinner! There are starving kids out there."
  - **Validating response:** "Honey, I'm sorry you don't like this dinner, and I see that you are really hungry." (*Don't worry. We'll cover the topic of respect and when and how to address disrespect later in the book. But first you need to set the foundation for connection. Remember: you are validating the child's *feelings*, not their disrespect.)
- Child: "My teacher is so annoying. I hate her."
  - **Ineffective response:** "It's time to grow up. I met her at a parent/teacher conference. She's not so bad."
  - **Validating response:** "I hate when teachers are annoying! It can be so frustrating having a teacher like that."

Validation should not come in the form of a question. When you ask questions like, "Why? What happened?", it can close the door of communication because it is too intrusive for children when they have big feelings. Tread lightly to keep them talking. If you dismiss their feelings, try to "fix" the problem, or come on too strong, they will stop talking. You simply need to be a good listener and empathize with them.

Think of a friend who "gets it" when you're upset, the one who always understands and doesn't judge. I'm lucky to have a friend like that. Whenever I call her to complain, she validates my feelings. "I hear you," she says. "I hate everyone too!" She's my favorite person to vent to. She's also the same person I call for advice when I'm done venting and ready to get real. Your children need you to be in their corner, to be that person who "gets it." It builds trust and keeps communication channels open.

After you validate, your children will most likely keep talking. Continue to be a good listener and show empathy. If they seem open to your advice, offer some guidance. If not, don't get discouraged. They may need some time to cool off. As long as your kids know you understand them and are there whenever they need support, you've done your job.

Vitamin B6: Positive Attention

It's important to give children positive attention, so they don't try to get noticed through negative means. Children who act out may be consciously—or subconsciously—trying to connect with you. After all, they *do* get your attention when they misbehave. Parents often make the mistake of ignoring their children when they are playing nicely and behaving. We stay quiet and enjoy those ten minutes of peace. But by giving your children positive attention in those moments, you will experience many more minutes of peace in the future.

Here are some examples of positive attention:
- "Honey, you're playing so nicely with your brother."
- "Joelle, you're waiting so patiently for your ice cream!"
- "Sam, wow! I noticed you listened on the first try when Mommy asked you to take a shower."
- "Jack, you're using such beautiful table manners!"
- "Sarah, I noticed you shared your candy with your sister. You're such a giver!"
- "Michelle, I noticed you didn't yell when your brother knocked down your tower but instead chose to use your words. You should be really proud of yourself."

Children like positive attention. It puts them on a track that leads to more appropriate behavior. By feeding them words of encouragement, you are filling their "emotional tanks."

Bottom line: If your children's emotional tanks aren't full, and they don't feel connected with you, that emotional void can lead to misbehavior.

Iron: Un-labeling

Children will always live up to their "label." If you label one child as "the difficult one," "the problem child," "the lazy one," etc., they will inevitably become that child. It's important that you separate your children from their actions. Just as a person struggling with addiction should not identify as an addict but a person who struggles with addiction, a child struggling to behave should not be labeled as a problem child but a child who is struggling to behave appropriately. When you address negative behavior, specify that the behavior is not a reflection of the child's inherent character. Negative labels put people in a box—a box that is hard to escape. When you separate your children from their actions, the message is clear: you don't see *them* in a negative light, just the behavior. That message runs deep. It's like saying, "This behavior is unbecoming of a child like you." It lets them know they are capable of behaving more appropriately. Labeling your children in a positive way—"You are such a giver!"—can change patterns and have a powerful, beneficial effect.

Vitamin D: Giving Children Independence through Choice and Space

- "Did you do your homework? Let me see it."
- "Did you complete your Lexia minutes? I have not seen you log on once this week."
- "Did you make your bed?"
- "When are you going to read your book for the book report? You know it's due on Monday, right?"

How many of us are constantly checking up on our kid's responsibilities? It's not that we are bored or have nothing better to do than micromanage their daily assignments; it comes from a place of being proactive. We just want to avoid the problems that come with giving children independence. We are worried that giving them that space may result in their messing up or not meeting their responsibilities. Ultimately, we don't want to receive an email from their teacher explaining her concerns about the three missing homework assignments that week. Where is the fine line between being overly involved and not being involved enough? Here's how I see it.

At each stage of a child's life, you need to evaluate what the child can manage on his or her own while pushing the line of assistance further and further away from the child. This means holding children responsible for completing tasks while responsibly teaching them the skills they need to get to the next level of independence. By keeping this goal in mind, you can slowly and effectively develop your children's autonomy and sense of responsibility as they grow up.

For example, let's say you start a conversation by telling your ten-year-old that you have a proposal. "I know I bug you a lot about completing your homework and chores, and I ask you too often if you've completed your responsibilities. I can see how that annoys you, and I feel there is a better way, one that will make you feel less stifled and help me feel more comfortable. So here's my idea: I'm going to leave you alone and not bug you anymore. I will simply write down a list of your responsibilities for the week and leave the timing up to you to get them done. Once the list is complete, please leave it on the kitchen counter, so I can see that you've checked off all your tasks. Then you are free to use your iPad and Xbox. What do you think of that plan?" (Parents don't usually allow iPads or electronics until homework is complete, so it makes sense to use this as motivation or a point of reference for timing.)

Then continue the conversation by using positive reinforcement. "Honey, I'm confident you will be able to manage your own schedule. I believe you are responsible enough to do so. However, if it becomes difficult to manage it on your own, and I get an email or a call from your teacher with concerns about missing assignments, I will have no choice but to intervene and help you. This is *not* a punishment; we just may need more time to learn these new time management skills and responsibilities. I know you would appreciate the space, and I think you are ready for this new independence in your life. How do you feel about it?"

Let's say the following week you get a call from your son's teacher explaining that he did not complete his homework for the week, even though he checked off the boxes of completed homework every night, knowing your plan was to not police him. You also made it crystal clear that he's responsible for his own choices, and that such privileges are earned by completing his tasks. So, you tell your son he didn't meet his responsibilities for the week, and because of *his* choice, you will now be helping him manage his time properly. You enforce the consequence—no iPad or Xbox—and explain that he will get his privileges back as soon as he has finished his missing assignments and that you will review his homework to confirm completion. You can cap off the discussion by saying this is not a punishment but a way to help him learn to manage his responsibilities. Express confidence that your son will learn this and check with him in a few weeks to try again.

Now let's talk about a child who isn't ready for the big step of managing his time and completing tasks independently. Remember that the goal is to set your kids up, so they can feel and be successful on their own. Instead of throwing the book at them and setting them up for failure with expectations that are too high, provide opportunities to accomplish more modest goals.

For example, imagine one of your children rarely comes home from school with the books she needs to do her homework. Come up with a plan for her to remember to bring home *one* book for the week. Discuss silly ideas for how she can remind herself to bring the book home. Allowing her to decide the most effective way to remember will motivate her for the task. Let's say the child suggests a Post-it note on her folder. Compliment her efforts: "Wow! That's a great idea to help as a reminder! I may use that for my own schedule. Should we decorate one together?" When she does remember that one book, praise her abilities and effort. "Wow! You should be proud of yourself. Look how you remembered to bring your book home on your own! I think you're ready for another responsibility. How about another Post-it for book number two? I believe you are super capable!" In this way, you can give the child tangible goals in stages that allow her to feel independently successful *and* capable. This will give her space to grow into a responsible adult.

Will it always be smooth sailing? Of course not. Even adults have trouble managing their time and responsibilities. But as long as you see improvement, you can support your children and adjust your expectations while continuing to move toward independence.

Why is it so important to teach your kids physical and emotional independence? Because it allows them to develop their personalities, learn the skills of time management and responsibility, experience natural consequences, and feel successful and capable about their accomplishments. It can be scary for parents to give their children the freedom to make their own choices because, inevitably, we will witness bad ones. But even bad choices are good for development. Some of the hardest lessons are learned through making bad choices. That doesn't mean letting your children run wild and hoping for the best. It means starting with small opportunities for your children to make responsible choices that grow into bigger and more frequent responsibilities.

To keep the balance between too much and too little autonomy, my rule of thumb is, as children demonstrate responsible behavior, they earn the reward of more independence. Take, for example, a twelve-year-old girl who asks her parents if she can walk to her friend's house by herself. Her parents feel she is ready and responsible enough to take this big step. The parents say yes while adding some rules: "Honey, this is a big step for all of us, and Mommy and I feel you are very responsible. But we have two rules. First, make sure to send us a text as soon as you get there. And we expect you home by five o'clock, before it gets dark outside." You cap it off by saying, "I hope this works out, so we can continue to give you the independence you would like in the future."

At a certain point, like it or not, you will lose control over the choices your children make. If your parenting approach isn't geared toward developing independence, this shift will happen abruptly without the proper preparation, and it will be more challenging for you and your children to adapt. The reality is that children are going to grow up and make their own choices—some good, some bad. Your role is to prepare them for adulthood with the skills they need to thrive. At the end of the day, all you can do as a parent is discuss responsibilities, assist with positive reinforcement, and hold your children accountable when they fall short.

Hovering. However well intentioned, parents who shadow their children's every move don't give them enough space to grow, which often limits their children's learning opportunities. This can stifle children and cause them to act out. Children learn through play and space, through failure and mistakes. If you're involved in every experience of your children's lives, they won't learn important skills that will allow them to navigate on their own one day. Finding the balance between setting boundaries and giving them some independence will pay many dividends later. A simple example of this for young children is allowing your child to walk ahead of you while instructing them to stop at the next tree.

The power of choices. Offering choices is a great way for children to demonstrate their independence within the boundaries you set. It allows you and your children to work together to meet their needs and yours. When children make their own choices, they feel empowered. By offering specific choices, parents give children *limited* control, space, and independence while remaining in command of the outcome.

Example #1: When a child wants to play before his homework is complete.

Child: "I want to play *now!*"

Mom: "I can see you are enjoying your down time. Do you want five more minutes of playtime?"

Child: "Yes."

Mom: "OK, but five minutes is the limit. If you stick to five minutes, I will offer this option whenever you need extra time before finishing your homework. However, if it's hard for you to stop playing after five minutes, we will have to go back to completing your homework before you can play with your toys."

The child's needs are validated, and mommy stays in control. Remember, children need to be able to predict the consequences of their choices. If the child doesn't cooperate after five minutes, you must follow through: "It looks like you weren't able to stick to the five-minute limit, so we'll have to wait a couple of weeks to try again."

Example #2: Bedtime

Mom: "Honey, do you want to wear your red pajamas or pink ones? It's your choice."

Child: "I don't want either."

Mom: "OK. You can take some time to decide."

Example #3: The hungry child

Mom: "Time for dinner!"

Child: "I want a snack."

Mom: "You can have a healthy snack like fruit or vegetables, or you can have a snack of your choice after dinner. It's up to you."

Omega 3: Becoming Educated on Developmental Stages

When parents know what to expect at certain stages of their children's lives, they are less likely to stress over their behavior. Not only will that allow you to take a deep breath, knowing your children are acting "age appropriate," more importantly, you can better support your children by understanding their needs. We all know the phrases "the terrible twos" and "typical teenager." Although difficult for parents, these are well-understood transitions. When your child is experiencing the terrible twos, for example, you aren't shocked by what you see, and you feel somewhat comforted knowing that you aren't the only parents who are dealing with tantrums at this stage. Likewise, when your teenager rolls his or her eyes, you aren't surprised because you know it is typical of adolescents. However, we rarely hear what to expect between the ages of two and adolescence, so gaining some insight into what your children are experiencing at these various stages can be really helpful for you and your children. By becoming educated on all such stages, you can better prepare mentally and become more emotionally well equipped to support your children by meeting their needs during each stage of their life.

Zinc: Clear Rules

It is often the case that the rules at home aren't clear—not to parents or their children. Before you can hold your children accountable, everyone needs to be clear on the rules. More importantly, your children need to be able to predict what will happen if they break a rule. Although each house will have a different set of rules, some form of rules must be in place to provide structure and security. I believe children should be involved in the process of establishing such rules, so everyone feels the rules are clear and fair for each member of the house. In my home, we have "family meetings" whenever we want to discuss or adjust the Gindi family rules.

A few weeks ago, I was reminded of how important it is for children to be clear on the rules. My family was invited to my cousin Freda's house. A few of her sisters were there along with their children. One of the cousins, Isaac, started throwing a tantrum because he wanted candy. His mom gave him what I like to call a "soft no." All the other kids were having a lollipop. She turned to me, the "parenting teacher," and asked for my advice. Her son is a smart, persistent three-year-old. I said, "Well, what's your rule about candy at home?"

"He doesn't have candy at home," she replied.

"OK, what is your candy rule when he goes out?"

"Sometimes I let him have a candy if the other kids are having some."

There was the problem.

I explained that her son had to be clear on the rules before she could implement them. The wishy-washy approach she described only encourages tantrums with the hope that mommy will give in. Soon after, my cousin took her son home and told him the new rule: "We don't eat candy in our house, but we never really talked about having candy at other people's homes. The new candy rule when we go to other people's houses is that you can have one candy, but only if the other kids are having a candy. If you ask for more candy after that, I will say no. If you get upset, Mommy will have to take you home, so we don't disturb the other people there."

When she told me this later, I suggested that she ask him to repeat the new rule back to her to ensure he understood it.

Prepare your children before a play date by role playing the issue you are working on. It's a very effective way of making rules more tangible. For example:

> Mom: "Honey, let's pretend we're at Jason's house, and I'm you and you're me."
> Mommy (the pretend child): "Thank you, Jason, for the lollipop. Mmmmm, it tastes soooo good! Can I have one more, Mommy?"
> Child (the pretend mommy): "Ha ha ha, nooo!"
> Mommy (the pretend child): "But whyyyyy? Wahhhhhh! I want one!"
> Child (the pretend mommy): "It's the rule, Jason. If you keep carrying on, we will have to go home."

Many parents are wish-washy even when they say "yes" to a child. It can come off as "Ahhhh . . . ummm . . . OK, fine." It's best, however, to emphasize your "yes" when you say it. It's another way of saying, "Of course, honey!" Your kids need to know that you love to say "yes" to them and don't like to say "no." It sends the message that when you say "no," it's because you love them, not because you want to make them miserable. Saying "yes" as often as possible will also make your "no" more impactful.

Vitamin E: Following Through

Following through happens in three stages:
- Your child is clear on the rules and the consequences in advance.
- If your child breaks the rule, you follow through on the consequences.
- When your child is calm, you validate his or her feelings and restate the rule.

The next time my cousin's son throws a tantrum for a second candy, if she doesn't honor the consequence and take him home out of respect to the others, he will learn that "Mommy caves in when I act up." The lessons about rules are always learned after the follow-through. When the child calms down, it's important to validate his or her feelings and then restate the rule. The conversation should be short and sweet. "Honey, I know you were upset that you didn't get the second candy, but the rule is one candy when we go to a friend's house. I hope that the next time we're there, we can stay longer to play." After a few follow-throughs, your child will learn that his efforts to manipulate, guilt trip you, or embarrass you will not result in your giving in, and the tantrums and outbursts will likely subside.

In their book, *Transforming the Difficult Child*, co-authors Howard Glasser and Jennifer Easley describe a man who doesn't care to follow the speed limit. "I simply go as fast as I please," he declares. Then one day he reads in the newspaper that the speed limits on the main road are going to be enforced. *Yeah, right, they are always saying that*, he thinks. The next day he gets pulled over. The officer says "Good morning" and hands him a ticket. However, the ticket is only a two-dollar fine, so the man continues to speed. Each time he speeds though, the same thing happens. His tickets begin piling up, and he becomes agitated. He tries to talk himself out of the next few tickets, but the officer will not give in. The man threatens, jokes, pleads, and even tries to bully the officer. He does everything he can to avoid getting the tickets, but each time the officer stays neutral and hands him a ticket. The officer may validate that the man is upset, but he still follows through with the consequence. Over time, the driver learns that when he speeds, he will get a ticket—no ifs, ands, or buts.

Following through is a must if you want to teach your children a lesson. If you want your children to honor a rule, you must be willing to act if they break it, so be careful what you commit to. If a rule is not well thought out, you may end up following through on a consequence that is too severe or impacts you as much as your children.

My rule of thumb is to give only one warning before following through on a consequence. The reason is that you don't want to encourage your children to listen to a request or command *eventually*. If your children are successful at continuing what they are doing, they will continue. The goal is to get them to listen on the first try. For example, a child is acting out at the dinner table. His parents ignore his behavior the first couple of times, but he is starting to frustrate everyone. Mom gives him a warning: "Honey, the next time you interrupt your siblings when they are speaking, you will need to leave the table for two minutes." The child interrupts again. Mom says, "I see you have chosen to leave the table for two minutes." She follows through by removing the child from the table.

II. THE TEACHER

Children often feel motivated to improve their behavior, but they lack the skills to do so. As parents, we have a responsibility to teach these skills to our children. These skills include communicating effectively, cultivating a "growth mindset," practicing tolerance and resiliency when faced with challenges, and becoming responsible members of society. These essential life skills will not only minimize the chaos and negativity that comes along with discipline, they will also help them throughout their lives.

Teaching Communication Skills

In today's world of nearly endless distraction, children are losing their ability to communicate verbally. They may want to communicate better, and they may be motivated to try, but they simply haven't learned the proper tools. Blame it on their phones and social media, but either way, now more than ever, children need to express themselves in a healthy and effective way to meet their needs. When they don't learn these skills, it can lead to emotional and psychological problems. Toddlers who don't know how to ask for something may resort to tantrums and take that strategy with them when they grow up. The following tips can get you started on teaching communication skills to your children.

- **Modeling:** As always, the first step in teaching effective communication skills is examining your own communication style. Parents who yell, nag, curse, demean, or shout from afar at their children are modeling that behavior for their kids. Instead, parents should focus on maintaining eye contact while speaking and communicate clearly, slowly, and respectfully. The children of parents who model healthy communication are better at communicating with others.
- **Building Language:** Children often have a hard time expressing themselves and labeling their feelings, which makes it more challenging for parents to support and communicate with them. Helping children find words to match their feelings will assist them in building communication skills. Here are some examples of how you can help your children develop language to identify feelings:
  - "You are so *frustrated*!"
  - "I can see how *upsetting* that was to you."
  - "It can feel *awkward* meeting new people."
  - "When Charlie grabbed your toy, you felt *angry*!"
  - "I noticed that you feel *uncomfortable* when Grandma kisses you."
  - "I can see you felt *embarrassed* when Jack said you don't know how to read."

One of my kids had what is called a "speech delay" in his early years—he had a hard time getting his words out. I decided to write flash cards with a different feeling on each card. Every time he was upset, he pointed to the feeling he was experiencing. It worked great. Once I knew how he was feeling, I was able to help him by validating his feelings and then asking him how we could work it out.

You can also build language in the way you express yourself to your children. For example, "Mommy felt really nervous when the school called me about what happened at recess."

- **Encourage Self-Expression:** Children should always feel comfortable expressing themselves and communicating their needs. The way they learn that is from how their parents respond to them. When your children do express themselves, compliment them on using their words, and give them your full attention.

Helpful Tip: My go-to phrase when a child screams, whines, or cries out for something they want is, "Try again." Once the child stops whining, I compliment him on using his "big boy" voice, and then I try to accommodate him. If he continues to whine, I simply say, "Mommy can't hear you when you speak that way. I'm ready to listen to you when you use your big boy voice." It's important that your children know they will not get your attention through negative channels because, inevitably, it will become a habit if it works.

Teaching a Growth Mindset

How do your children respond to failure and disappointment? Do they shy away from things they aren't good at? Do they run away from difficult tasks? More importantly, do they allow failure and difficulty to define their abilities? For example,

- "I'm not a math person. Never was, never will be."
- "I failed the test because I'm stupid."
- "I'm just not good at sports."

Maybe they face failure and disappointment in a different way by not allowing negative outcomes to define them. They persevere in the face of difficulty. They try harder. They learn from it and move forward with healthy affirmations.

- "I'm not good at math yet."
- "I failed the test, but if I study harder and pay more attention in class, I will do better."
- "I'm learning how to play sports."

In her book, *The Growth Mindset*, Carol Dweck discusses the power of acquiring such an outlook on life. People with a growth mindset believe they aren't bound by their genes. They know their abilities can be developed. Why does this matter? Because this perspective allows us to grow, learn, and persevere through difficulties. Without a growth mindset, we allow failure to paralyze us. We miss out on opportunities to evolve and reach our potential. We need to abandon the limitations of a fixed mindset and walk the path of a growth mindset by recognizing that we are capable of change and growth.

I took a lot of time thinking about these ideas and did some self-reflecting. Why did I see myself as a failure in school? Why did I think I wasn't capable of doing better? It wasn't until I reached adulthood that I found confidence in my abilities. What changed? I shifted from a fixed mindset to a growth mindset.

Growing up, we were judged to be either smart or stupid—at least according to whatever test was being used to measure a particular ability. Such tests didn't consider learning disabilities or accommodate children who needed explanations or help. Teachers were not allowed to answer any questions during a test. You can imagine how anxious and helpless the "stupid" children (like me!) felt when faced with an exam. My mother tried her best to advocate for me. She even asked the principal to give me more time to take the tests, and he agreed. The problem was, I'm the fastest test taker in the world, and I still am! One afternoon I sat at my desk for forty minutes just twiddling my thumbs. More time wasn't the answer; my problem was focus. But I didn't say anything. When I came home with my grade—whatever it was—my mother always said, "You did great, honey!" I never knew if that was true, but her support always felt good.

While writing this book, I realized I had somehow developed a growth mindset over the years. How did that happen? For one, I learned from experience that people cannot be measured by a test. I learned that the "stupid" kids were not actually stupid. Many of them went on to become quite successful. I was also lucky enough to have been surrounded by people who believed in me and looked at me with pride and joy. Plus, I married a man who saw me the same way. My husband and I got married while I was getting my associate degree in college. Whenever I had trouble with assignments, he'd say, "Well, you never learned about that." I took comfort in knowing there *was* a way forward. It was called "learning." From that point on, I continued my journey through school with a growth mindset. I was no longer anxious; I was simply learning. Isn't that what school is for? I must have skipped the neuro-psych evaluation and used trial and error to figure out the most effective ways for me to study, write, and focus. It turned out that I was a good listener and rarely needed to take notes.

During my first semester back from getting married, my English literature professor assigned the class to write an essay on the quote, "Beauty is in the eye of the beholder." I will never forget it. It was right up my alley. Finally, an assignment about psychology! I enjoyed every minute of writing it and earned an "A." The professor told me I had talent and then walked away. That experience was pivotal because it led me to realize the power of a growth mindset. The second I let go of the limited mindset, "I'm not a good student," I was able to become a good student. This professor wouldn't remember me if he saw me again, but I certainly remember him. And I still have that essay.

Translating a Growth Mindset into Parenting

Developing a growth mindset is a powerful tool when it comes to learning how to navigate through failure and difficulties. When people realize they can improve in areas they wish to, they will have an easier time coping because they know they control their next steps forward. They have the power to change their situation. Parents play an important role in helping children develop a growth mindset. Here are a few ways you can help your children in this regard.

Model a growth mindset. A simple shift in how you see failure and disappointment will show your children how to cope with such things and pave the way for them to embody that perspective. When a child comes home with a bad grade on a test, evaluate your feelings about it before responding. Do you see your child as incapable and stupid? Or do you see an opportunity for growth and hope there is one last math test so your child can redeem himself or herself? Perspective matters. So does the way you respond to failure and difficulty. How you talk to yourself and your children when faced with failure and mistakes matters. Do you model anxiousness and avoidance or a growth mindset? Consider the following examples.

- Vivian asks her mom if they can bake challah for Shabbat together. "I have never made challah before," her mom says, "but I always wanted to learn. Let's do it!"
- Mommy is on the phone with a friend who asks her to come to a new exercise class. Mommy says, "I feel uncomfortable going because I don't know how to do Zumba, but if I go to the class, I can learn. I'll never know if I don't try!"
- Mommy says, "I lost in tennis today. I played against a strong group of girls. I know I'm not on their level yet, but I'll get there if I keep playing."

When my daughter was six, I asked if she wanted to play tennis. She told me, "No. I'm not good at it." I sat her down and asked, "How can you be good if you never play it?" I also asked if she thought I would waste money on lessons if she was already a great tennis player. We discussed how she might feel embarrassed if she didn't hit the ball over the net and the importance of trying new things and not worrying about how to play but how fun it may be to learn. I told her about my first experience playing tennis: I served the ball, hit my leg with the bottom of my racquet, and ended up with a huge bruise. We both laughed and agreed that after she learned how to play, she'd have the option to quit. I wanted her to learn that abilities develop through effort and practice, and while she would experience uncomfortable feelings, she would also have a chance to learn the gifts of coping and perseverance. She is now ten years old and playing tennis every week!

Understanding the brain. Why do children have such a hard time regulating their emotions? How do you dialogue with your children when they are dealing with big feelings? How can you help your children learn how to cope with difficult situations?

In their book, *The Whole-Brain Child*, Daniel J. Seigel and Tina Payne Bryson address these important questions by providing insight into how the brain functions. In short, the brain is divided into two hemispheres, left and right. The left side is in charge of logical thought, and the right side processes emotions and feelings. When the two sides are integrated, we are able to process our emotions, make sense of them, and regulate our behavior. Children usually operate from the right side of their brain. This state of mind is rarely logical and rational. "Mom, you never let me jump off my bed, so I can learn how to fly. I hate you!" As parents, we often respond to the right side of our children's brains with our left side, using logic and rationale. "Honey, you can't jump off the bed! Humans can't fly, and Mommy doesn't want you to get hurt." The problem is that when we don't acknowledge the feelings that are consuming them, we hit an "unresponsive right-brain brick wall."

The authors discuss a more effective approach they call "Connect and Redirect." It is far more effective, they say, to meet children in their state of mind by first connecting and validating their feelings. "Honey, I can see how badly you want to fly. It would be really cool to fly, right?" The goal is for the child to "feel felt." After we connect to the child's state of mind by acknowledging their feelings, we can then redirect—a process of integrating both sides of the brain by introducing logic. This lays the foundation of healthy coping skills by giving children the ability to integrate emotions and logic: "Although Mommy understands you really want to learn how to fly, it's just too dangerous to jump off your bed. Mommy needs to keep you safe." Once you recognize the dominance of the right brain in your children's behavior, you can help them learn to self-regulate and develop healthy coping skills.

Coping skills. Watching your child go through a difficult time can be just as painful for you as it is for the child. As a parent, my instinct to jump in and try to rescue my kids from negative feelings and situations. The problem is, difficult situations are inevitable. Although we would like to think we will always be around when our children go through them, the reality is that we won't. That is why learning how to tolerate and manage through difficult times is invaluable.

There are two types of coping skills: skills that focus on coping through difficult emotions and skills that focus on dealing with a problem and working toward a solution. Here are some tips on teaching children how to cope with difficult emotions:

- **Allow all feelings.** "It's OK to be angry. It's OK to be sad. It's OK to feel hurt. It's OK to feel disappointed." People tend to avoid negative feelings simply because it can be painful to experience them. When it comes to learning coping skills, though, those uncomfortable feelings should not be dismissed. Sitting with your feelings will enable you to move through them. Ironically, negative emotions are not always negative; they can help you change a behavior that may not be working well for you. It's true for adults, and it's true for kids. This process of self-awareness and acceptance is a powerful tool that parents can teach their children.

- **Provide a supportive environment.** When your children are dealing with big feelings, consider the home environment that surrounds them. Providing an environment that embraces *all* feelings creates the conditions for open communication—the tool that allows us to meet our children in their emotional state and help them make sense of their feelings. Your response to "heightened" feelings will affect your children's ability to self-regulate. That response will either help your children or add to their feeling of being overwhelmed. Studies show that when people are face to face, they start to synchronize with and mirror each other, so be mindful of your response. Children need to feel safe with their feelings. They need to know that whatever they are feeling, they have a secure and comfortable environment that still embraces them.

- **Model coping skills.** Children learn most powerfully from what we do, not from what we say. Modeling what it looks like to manage feelings when someone is upset is probably the most tangible way for children to learn how to deal with difficult situations. If mommy is a ticking time bomb, her child learns that when his feelings are too big to manage, he, too, can explode. If daddy shuts down when things get tough, his daughter may learn to keep her feelings inside. It is thus especially important to take a hard look at how you respond to difficult situations and model the right way to act even when *you* are upset.

- **Be proactive.** Having a plan in place for when things get tough. Talk to your children about how to assist them when they are dealing with big feelings. Explore ways of helping your children before they get reactive. "Honey, when Mommy sees you getting really upset, what can I do to help you calm down? Maybe we can make a space for you to go for a little while until you are ready to talk about it." Teach them how to manage their frustrations by exploring solutions together.

- **Explore different strategies.** When trying to help your child manage their feelings, don't be afraid to try different strategies. Depending on their age, consider taking advantage of a calm moment to brainstorm with your child various tools that they can use when distressed. Hold their hand while exploring different ideas. For younger children, I suggest creating a "calm down" activity list when they are overwhelmed with big feelings. As adults, we have many options for getting through a difficult time: taking a walk or doing other exercise, deep breathing, writing our feelings in a journal, a long shower, watching a funny movie, talking to a friend, or simply crying it out. For older children, having a plan can help them better prepare for anxious situations. For example, "Honey, finals are coming up. I know it can be a really stressful time. Let's talk about different things we can do to manage next week, so you are able to get through it." Working with them to create what works will lead to invaluable tools for coping with the inevitable ups and downs of life.
- **Code red.** If your children have a hard time expressing themselves when angry, come up with a code word they can use when they are ready to explode. My son came up with "Red!" Whenever he screamed "Red," I went to him immediately and followed through with our plan, which meant I carried him to another room where he screamed into a pillow for a few minutes. We discussed the problem after he calmed down.
- **Timing.** When you notice your child is having a difficult time, try to intervene before the child escalates: "Honey, I can see it's hard for you to handle that. Mommy is here to help you."
- **Validate your child's feelings.** "Honey, I can see that you are very angry right now." "Honey, I can see you are angry that your sister played with your toy." Validating will help dial down your child's anger.
- **Limits are good.** Empathize but set limits on acting out of anger. Establish clear rules. No destructive behavior. Hitting is unacceptable. Remember, you can validate their feelings and disapprove of a behavior at the same time.

- **An ounce of prevention.** Help your child learn problem-solving skills to avoid becoming angry in the first place. For example, help them express their needs with words, not by yelling and acting out.
- **Learn their triggers.** What sets them off? Hunger? Exhaustion? Can you change your schedule to allow for calm-down time after school or camp?
- **Daily nutrition.** Revisit the "vitamins" above to make sure they are getting their daily dose.

Here are some tips on teaching children how to cope with a problem:
- Don't dismiss negative emotions. Allow your children to experience them.
- Discuss their problem.
- Help your children name the emotion(s) they are feeling.
- Work with your children to learn from their experience and explore ways of avoiding the action or behavior that led to those negative emotions. For example, it may be constructive to explore setting boundaries with a person or avoiding certain situations that result in hurtful feelings.
- Discuss possible outcomes from such coping strategies, both positive and negative.
- If a child is the legitimate victim of an event he or she had no control over, validate and empathize with the child. Teach him or her what can be learned from that experience.

Learning from negative experiences helps us develop proactive approaches and get better results in the future. Difficult situations have much to teach us!

Teaching Responsibility

> Mom: "Shower time."
> Child: "No! I'm not taking a shower."
> Mom: "It's 9 p.m.! I'm giving you ten more minutes, and then you're taking a shower."
> REPEAT.

How can you teach your children to carry out their responsibilities? For some children, even the simplest tasks like taking a shower at a reasonable time can be a problem. Why can't they just do what they are supposed to do?

Sometimes it's as simple as putting your foot down. At other times you may find yourself in a pattern of constantly reminding and threatening. Some children will ask for a few more minutes and comply after you've given them that time. Others will keep asking for more and more time or just refuse. Depending on the child's age, the circumstances, and the importance, your approach will be different.

Teaching your children to be responsible gives them another tool for becoming successful in life. It will take effort, patience, practice, and discipline, but like everything else discussed in this book, it will be worth the effort.

Provide routine and structure. When children have a routine and a structure, repetitive tasks become easier to manage, and they will develop successful habits.

Avoid giving orders. Don't say, "Go brush your teeth!" or "Do your homework!" Instead, list your children's responsibilities for the night and then ask them to choose the order and make their own schedule. "Honey, there are three things on the to-do list tonight: dinner, shower, and homework. You choose the order, and when all your responsibilities are finished, you can use your iPad." The goal is not to control your children but to help them develop their own initiative on meeting their responsibilities.

Use positive reinforcement. Say things like, "Nice job following through on that," "I can see you stayed on task tonight," and "You are demonstrating such responsible behavior."

Hold them accountable. Part of your children learning to fulfill their responsibilities comes from being held accountable when they don't. That means setting clear rules and consequences. If a child refuses to complete his or her assignments, removing certain privileges—including those such as watching television and buying new sneakers—may be necessary to teach the child that privileges are earned by honoring commitments. (Refer to "The Consequence" below for more on this.)

Positive expectations. Many parents don't realize that much of the resistance associated with responsibilities is a result of their approach, which often comes in the form of a demand or a threat, however subtle. Children can easily sense such negative vibes and will run for the hills if they can. When it comes to responsibilities, your efforts should focus on making the child's experience more pleasant.

A mother called to ask me how to get her kids to help her with daily chores. It's a question I hear often and one that I'm fluent in answering.

Unfortunately, the word "chores" usually has a negative connotation. Speaking of which, have you ever said something like the following? "How many times do I need to tell you to put away your books?" "I'm not your slave!" "I'm not buying you any more clothes because they're always on the floor!"

If you remove the negativity that surrounds the word "chores" and replace it with a more positive expectation, you can begin the process of encouragement. How? By using chores as an opportunity to connect with your children and make them feel valuable. When children feel like they are part of a common goal and see chores as a time to connect with the family, they are more motivated to help. For example, when you ask a child to set the table for dinner while you empty the dishwasher, and you use that time to talk, laugh, and catch up, it becomes a different experience. What will work for your child? My "inner child" likes to listen to music when I'm working around the house. It calms me down and adds a bounce to my step!

This approach can be applied to any area that has become a little negative. With some creativity, effort, and patience, homework time, bath time, and dinner time can all turn into more positive experiences. For example, I noticed that homework was becoming a bad experience for my son and I because I was constantly reminding him to sit down and focus. I decided to change my approach and make the experience more positive. Knowing that my son likes to move around a lot, I decided to redirect him in a more structured way that would allow for both movement and homework. I suggested that he do some jumping jacks between math questions. He loved the idea! While the assignment took a little longer to complete, it was worth it because the negativity surrounding homework time has gradually disappeared.

The bottom line is that any "negative task" can be transformed into a more positive experience. Get creative, and remove the foreboding energy. Once that negativity diminishes, your children will have a better attitude when it comes to fulfilling their responsibilities.

The reality check. While these ideas may lead to improvement in helping your children be more responsible in certain areas, not all children will respond the same way. Some will simply hate doing what they need to do. However, that is unacceptable. Children need to learn that while we will encourage them and offer assistance, they will ultimately be held responsible for meeting their responsibilities.

III. CONSEQUENCES

OK, you've filled your children's emotional tanks and taught them the skills they need to improve their behavior. The final question is, when and how do you need to get involved when your children misbehave?

When Not to Get Involved: Natural Consequences

Natural consequences are the easiest way for children to learn from their experiences without outside intervention. Whenever you have an opportunity to allow your children to make a mistake, the learning that follows is always very effective. For example:

- If your child keeps forgetting his lunch, the natural consequence would be that your child will get hungry. If you don't intervene, your child will remember his lunch in the future.
- If your child refuses to wear a coat, allow her to be cold.
- If your child doesn't put his clothes in the hamper, they don't get cleaned.
- If your child refuses to do his homework, he gets in trouble in school.
- If your child doesn't study for her test, she will fail.

Isn't this how adults learn—or how they should learn? If we don't get enough sleep, we are tired during the day. If we skip breakfast, we are hungry. If we speed, we get a ticket.

A mother was having the "homework battle" with her son every night. I decided to help her end this battle once and for all by advising her to tell her son that she would no longer force him to do his homework. I told her to tell him that it was fine by her if he wanted to skip it, and she hoped his teacher understood. That night, her son didn't do his homework. She held her tongue and put my number on speed dial. I continued to calm her and advise her. Later that night, she sent his teacher an email explaining the problem she was having and that she'd support whatever the teacher needed to do to hold him responsible for not doing his homework. The next day, her son came home from school and started his homework right away. She didn't ask what happened or why the sudden change in behavior. She simply offered to help him if he needed it. The teacher emailed her that night and said she had given him the option to complete the assignment during recess, at home after school, or during the next day's recess. He chose to complete it at home. A few mornings later, I received a beautiful bouquet of flowers with a card saying, "Thank you! You saved my life." This mom was bravely willing to step aside and allow her son to learn a life lesson. *She* deserved the beautiful flowers, not me.

When you intervene in the process of natural consequences, the lesson is lost. You create a power struggle. If you tell your child, "I told you so" or "This is what happens when . . .," it will only create resentment, rebellion, revenge, refusal, a sense of inadequacy, and most importantly, the loss of a learning experience. So, bite your tongue when the world has provided your children with feedback that they did not meet expectations or do things the right way. Even though you predicted the outcome and want your kids to listen to you, the ultimate goal is for them to make smart decisions without your input—to learn from their own experiences. Your only job is to validate their feelings and show empathy.

When to Get Involved: Logical Consequences

Sometimes it's necessary to address inappropriate behavior by taking stronger action. How to approach and enforce logical consequences will depend on the age and maturity of your children.

Remember: consequences are not a way to punish children. They are a way to teach them. To ensure that your consequences are logical and effective, they need to pass the "Three Rs" test.

- **Reasonable:** The consequence must be fair in the eyes of the child and the parent.
- **Relatable:** The consequence needs to relate to the behavior.
- **Respectful:** The consequence must not be delivered through blame, shame, or disrespect.

Here are some examples of logical consequences.

- If a child spills his cereal, the reasonable and relatable consequence is for him to clean up the mess. If the message isn't delivered in a respectful way, and the child feels embarrassed or hurt, it will encourage negative attention, create resentment, and ultimately lead to more misbehavior.
- If an older child breaks a vase while throwing a ball, he should pay for it to be replaced. Deliver the message respectfully without making it personal. "Honey, I appreciate your apology, but the vase still needs to be replaced. I can help you come up with ideas on how you can earn enough money to do that." If he's not earning money yet, provide opportunities for him to do so. Offer some jobs around the house, or ask a neighbor if they need a housework helper or a weed puller.
- If a child uses her iPad when she's not supposed to, she loses the iPad for the day.

- If a teen stays out after curfew on Saturday night, she loses the privilege of going out the following Saturday night.
- If a child plays with toys, he needs to put them away. If he chooses not to, take the toys away for a few days. The respectful way of delivering that message is, "Honey, the rule is, we play, we put away. (I got that line from *Supernanny*, a British reality show). If you don't put your toys away when you are done playing, I will have to take them away for a few days."

Here are some examples of unrelatable/unreasonable consequences.
- A child spills his cereal—has to go to bed early. (Unrelatable)
- A child breaks a vase—is grounded for a month. (Unreasonable)
- A child uses her iPad—her new bike is returned. (Both)
- A teen stays out past curfew—his cell phone is taken away for a month. (Unreasonable)

Here are some examples of a disrespectful delivery.
- A child spills some cereal: "This happens *every single meal!* I am not cleaning up your spill again! I've had it with cleaning up after you."
- A child breaks a vase: "You are *so* clumsy. How many times are you going to break things in this house? I'm sick of it. You're going to pay for it."
- A child uses her iPad without permission: "I cannot believe you! You think you're still getting your new bike after what you just did? Think again."
- A teen stays out past curfew: "Enough is enough! You can't be trusted to follow the rules or to be responsible."

Remember: discipline should never be personal, or the lesson will get lost. Parents often try to demonstrate control when imposing consequences. We like to show our kids who's boss and send the message that, "You have to do what I say, or else." When you approach discipline as a means of making your children submit to you, we need to recognize that your ego is getting in the way, and you are hurting your children in the long run. On the other hand, if you show empathy while teaching them responsibility, it will preserve their dignity and allow them to right their wrong. "Firm and nice" is the way to go when delivering consequences.

It can be hard to come up with the perfect 3-R consequence "in the moment" because when you're upset, you may not be thinking clearly. That's why it is so important to take time to calm down first. Not only will this create a space to think, it also sets a good example for your children on how to deal with big feelings. After you calm down, you will be in a better position to address the child without compromising your relationship.

One day while pregnant with my second daughter, I brought my oldest daughter to the store. She was only two at the time but acted more mature than a five-year-old. I warned her in advance that we were only running in to get one item for the house and firmly stated that we wouldn't be buying any toys. Lo and behold, she found the one toy in the store, and it cost thirty dollars. I knew if I bought it, I'd be creating a monster because I had already told her the rule. So I said no, and she promptly laid on the floor and started screaming. Because of my pregnancy, I couldn't lift her up and leave. Mortified, I stood there on the verge of tears while other customers looked on. A few minutes later—what felt like hours to me—one of the staff helped me carry her to the car.

Still crying, I called my parenting teacher. She calmed me down and taught me an important lesson. When children go into a tantrum, people aren't looking at the child; they're looking at the parent's reaction. Like always, she was right. So, I came up with a plan that falls in line with the 3 R'S. I did not have a conversation with my daughter that night, nor did I punish her. I was too emotional for that. Instead, I pretended that nothing had happened. The next day I told her I was going to the store, and I wished I could bring her with me, but after what happened the previous day, I thought it best that she stay home with the babysitter. She freaked out, which I expected. I walked out as she hung from the back of the door, wailing, her feet literally off the ground. I got in my car and drove around the block twice. (I told the babysitter in advance about my plan.) I came home to find her in the same position. I told her that I missed having her with me and that I hoped she could come with me next time. Relatable, reasonable, respectful. She is now thirteen. I have never had to teach her that lesson again.

Arguments

Despite our best intentions, discipline can get ugly:

> Child: "Can I sleep at my friend's house tonight?"
> Mom: "No, honey. There are no sleepovers on a school night."
> Child: "But my friends are all sleeping there! Pleeeassse!"
> Mom: "No."
> Child: "You're so mean! You never let me do *anything*!"

Mom: "Honey, I'm sorry you're upset, but this is the rule."
Child: "Pleeeaasse! It's not fair!"

Smart moms walk away and don't engage past this point.

Once a rule is established, it takes two to argue. By simply saying— nicely and respectfully—"The answer is no. There are no sleepovers on a school night," you refuse to engage in the argument. When a child doesn't accept the answer, he or she will likely start an argument in the hope of getting the desired answer. At this point, you should just go about your business. By refusing to engage, you will, over time, teach your children that arguing doesn't work, and they shouldn't waste their time. (**Tip:** Don't take any phone calls during this time; it may create more frustration in the child.)

If you're not clear on whether you should make an exception, tell your child that you need some time to think, and you will come back to the situation with a clear answer. You don't want to get into the habit of saying "No" and then giving in. This will teach your children that arguing is the way to get what they want. If you find you are making a lot of exceptions in a particular area, adjust the rule. For example, "Honey, Daddy and I see you really want to start having sleepovers. We feel you are responsible enough, and we want you to be happy, so we are making a new rule. You are allowed to have one sleepover a month on the weekends."

As you begin to incorporate this new approach, your children will need time to adjust and will likely continue to make their case to get what they want. A cousin of mine has a nice analogy for this concept. She says it's like "sleep training" a baby. The first time you try, the baby will cry for thirty minutes. The second time, it will be for twenty minutes. And so on. Stay calm, and be patient. In time, children will learn that arguing is not an effective strategy.

Lying

The topic of lying is especially sticky when it comes to discipline.

Mom: "Did you hit your brother?"
Child: "No! He's lying."
Mom: "Then why does he have a mark on his arm?"
Child: "Because he always rubs it to get me into trouble."
Mom: "You aren't telling the truth. Go to your room!"

The question to ask is, "What would happen if the child was telling the truth?" You guessed it: he would probably get sent to his room. So, why would he tell the truth if the outcome is the same? Kids lie to avoid disapproval and punishment. They rely on the hope that you won't catch them. How, then, can you encourage truth telling? By *not* punishing your children when they tell the truth. "But Norma, he lied!", you may say. Yes, he did, but let me explain.

The fact is, all children lie. But if your child is afraid to tell you the truth, it will only hurt them in the future by not allowing them to come to you when they are in trouble. If you believe that the purpose of consequences is to teach, then you can teach your child to tell the truth by explaining that telling the truth is a better choice. We refrain from a consequence because we don't want that message to get lost in the child's reaction to the consequence. For example, "If you tell the truth, you won't be punished unless you have hurt or endangered others. Mommy always wants you to feel comfortable telling me when you do something wrong, so I can be there for you and help you figure it out." You can also instill the value of being truthful by giving your kids books about honesty and integrity. It's a great way for them to learn about telling the truth and the negative effects of lying. (I personally recommend *Eli and His Little White Lie* by Goldie Golding.) You can also use "natural consequences" with children who are chronically dishonest by letting them know it will be difficult for you to trust their words in the future when it really matters.

The Importance of Discipline

To all the parents who are reading this chapter and thinking, "None of this pertains to me because I am easy on my kids and rarely discipline," the following paragraph is for you.

"Permissive parenting" is a strategy I am quite familiar with. It characterizes a home that doesn't have much in the way of rules, structure, order, or discipline, in part because it's much easier for parents to say "Yes" to a child than "No." A permissive parenting approach sounds like a happy home—and that can certainly be the case. But if you want your children to learn essential life skills such as self-discipline, tolerance, respect, responsibility, hard work, accountability, social skills, appropriate behavior, persistence, coping skills, and problem-solving skills, they need rules and discipline. Discipline gets a bad rep, but if done correctly, it's an expression of love and commitment. Investing your time to teach morals, values, and responsibility to your children is the definition of true love, and it is often through discipline that you can instill these principles. Discipline helps children learn how to manage their behavior, so they can acquire the skills and tools they need to succeed in the real world.

Some Final Tips on Discipline

- Choose your battles.
- Implement a consequence only when you are prepared to follow through on it.
- Refrain from yelling, embarrassing, nagging, begging, and asking.
- Avoid repeated warnings.
- Be specific about what you are asking your child to do. For example, instead of saying, "Clean up your mess," be more specific: "Please put away your blocks."
- Anticipate a problem, and prepare for it. For example: Last night you told your child that she would not be able to use her iPad the following night. Gear yourself up for a more challenging night. Organize yourself as much as possible before the child comes home, and leave your schedule open because chances are you will not have time to deal with other things.
- Always remember to give your kids their "vitamins" because discipline without a relationship doesn't work and may actually result in more behavioral issues.
- When dealing with a strained relationship, always work toward rebuilding trust with your child, and do your best to refrain from disciplining until the relationship improves.

Some Common Misconceptions about Discipline

- "My kids only listen when I scream, yell, or punish."
- "My children will not do as they are told if I don't discipline or threaten them with a consequence."
- "But Norma, screaming and yelling work."

Yes, screaming, yelling, threatening, and "rushing to consequence" may work in the moment, but it comes with a heavy price tag. These responses don't address the emotional roots of the behavior and might result in other negative behaviors. There are no shortcuts in parenting, and any book that gives you an immediate solution is only addressing short-term cooperation. To change a behavior, children need to learn that the behavior is wrong, develop skills to incorporate an appropriate behavior instead, and practice it until it finally changes. This process takes time and effort from parents and children.

Quotes to Hold On To

"Rules without Relationship = Rebellion
Relationship without Rules = Chaos
Relationship + Rules = Respect + Responsibility"
—Josh McDowell (author and speaker)

"The level of cooperation parents get from their children is usually equal to the level of connection children feel with their parents."
—Pam Leo (independent scholar in human development, parent educator, certified childbirth educator, and a doula)

"When little people are overwhelmed by big emotions, it is our job to stay calm, not join their chaos."
—L.R. Knost (award-winning author, social justice activist, and family counselor)

6

Rivalry

Without fail, by mid-week I would be looking forward to a "cozy" weekend catching up on some sleep and organizing for the upcoming week. I would fantasize about the home-cooked Shabbat meal on Friday night, the beautiful nap I was going to take on Saturday, the new book I would read after my nap, and my cozy Sunday preparing my schedule, menu, and grocery list. Then I would wake up to reality. My beautiful Friday night dinner was full of arguments between my children. My Saturday nap was interrupted by more bickering, and my cozy Sunday looked more like the aftermath of a natural disaster. By Saturday afternoon, I was praying for Monday again.

Is this the way it has to be? Do we need to wait until our kids are out of the house to enjoy a peaceful weekend? Since the culprit, more often than not, was sibling rivalry, I decided to take it on and try to reclaim my weekends. I can't yet say my weekends are all cozy now, but I don't have to look forward to Monday anymore for relief. It has taken some work, but it's possible.

If you think about it, children join a family without the consent of their older siblings. Although parents may consider their other children in a decision to expand the family, the decision is ultimately made by the parents. Let's take a moment to process this. You give birth to your second child, bring your new baby home from the hospital, and announce to your older child, "This is your new sister!"

Your first child—let's call him David—isn't really sure what to make of this new human. During the first few weeks, you and your husband are exhausted and disheveled. You barely get dinner on the table, and the baby is always crying. David begins to wonder if this new human can be returned but then remembers that Mommy always says how cute and wonderful the baby is.

A few months pass, and now the baby is making weird sounds and moving around on the floor, and everyone gets excited about each little thing. Next the baby is touching David's toys, although Mommy and Daddy keep telling him she doesn't know what she's doing and that he needs to share those toys. David didn't ask for this new sibling, and now she's starting to agitate him. David may wonder if his parents want to replace him. Is this baby cuter than him? Why is she getting all their attention?

We rarely think about the thoughts that run through children's minds when we introduce them to a new member of the family. I once heard a great analogy about this experience. Imagine you come home to your husband holding a woman's hand. "This is my new wife!" He explains that you are still his wife, but he wanted a second wife. He encourages you to share your clothes and jewelry with her. He is constantly taking pictures of her and smiles whenever she does anything ordinary. You tell him you do not like this new wife of his, but you know it's too late; he already loves her. He reassures you that she's great (and that he still loves you!) and that, over time, you will realize she is the best gift he ever brought home for you.

Now we can begin to understand the psychology behind sibling rivalry. It may take a lot of adjusting, but with a little help and effort, children can learn to appreciate their siblings without having to wait until adulthood. Having a brother and/or sister (or more than one) can be one of the greatest blessings in this world.

Start managing sibling rivalry by addressing how to prevent it from happening in the first place. For example, help each of your children feel special by highlighting their positions in the family. What makes them unique? How do they contribute to the family?

- Do not compare your children to each other.

- Do not show favoritism.
- Provide clear rules.
- See your kids with fresh eyes.
- Teach communication skills.
- Teach problem-solving skills
- Provide "special sibling activities."

Making Each Child Feel Secure in Their Position in the Family

Take the analogy in the paragraph above. Imagine your husband brings home a second wife and explains that you will always be his first wife, he loves you unconditionally, and even though you may feel his attention is elsewhere at times, you are always on his mind. The new wife, he says, will never be able to replace you. As time passes, you realize that you and your husband are still very connected, and even though he shares time with his other wife, you are so secure in your relationship that you feel content. I realize that for adults, this sounds too unlikely to be true, but when it comes to the relationship between a parent and a child, it's quite possible. If a child knows that he—and only he—brings something to the family that no one else can, he will be more secure in his position. As noted in the chapter on self-esteem, children need to feel special. They need to know they cannot be replaced, that they are the piece that completes the family puzzle. No two pieces are the same, so there is no need to compete to protect their place in the puzzle.

Do Not Compare Your Children—Period

To illustrate this, let's return to the second wife analogy: "Honey, Jane is such an awesome cook. You should learn from her." "Honey, maybe if you exercise like Jane does, you won't be so tired all the time." "Honey, whenever I ask Jane to play tennis with me, she always says yes." "Why can't you be a little easier going like Jane?" If this happened, Jane's picture would end up on the front cover of the *New York Post* with the title, "The Murder of Jane: A Family Tragedy." Doing the same sort of thing to your children will fuel similar feelings of resentment.

Do Not Show Favoritism

We all have one child who melts our heart. The child who is easy going, who doesn't argue with us, who feels for us when we're upset, who can do no wrong. Your relationship with that child is obvious to the rest of the family. The other children are constantly saying, "You never punish him" or "You favor him" or "He always gets whatever he wants." As parents, we know we love *all* our children. However, we love our children in different ways because they are all different. Some children are easier by nature, and naturally there will be less confrontation with them. But that shouldn't translate into favoritism.

To distinguish favoritism from deferential treatment, you need to learn to appreciate and accept each of your children's personalities. It's your job to make each of your children feel important in their position in the family *and* in your heart. Children should never feel threatened or overshadowed by the ease of your other relationships but secure and confident in their relationship with you. That means you must connect with all your children regardless of how hard it may be at times. You need to focus on building such a relationship, especially with those children who are more difficult to connect with. A major cause of sibling rivalry is the lack of emotional connection between a parent and their "difficult" child. Each child needs to have a full emotional tank in order to avoid the jealousy that is at the root of sibling rivalry.

Establish Clear Rules

As I've discussed, children need to be able to predict the consequences of their actions. If children aren't clear on the rules, it creates a space for argument, manipulation, and guilt. On the other hand, providing clear rules sets the tone for fairness and helps you remain firm and consistent in your approach.

Rules need to be enforced across the board for each child in the family. If every child is held responsible for breaking the rules, it will prevent negative feelings of injustice, jealousy, and favoritism. Although consequences will vary for each child according to age and disposition, they need to be implemented consistently whenever the children break a rule. (And as long as the rules are logical, they will usually fit the misbehavior.) For example, a fourteen-year-old cannot be put in a time out, and you cannot take the car keys away from a two-year-old. It's also not uncommon to be more lenient when disciplining younger children. In fact, parents are usually much harder on the oldest child. I once heard the phrase, "Treat the oldest like the youngest and the youngest like the oldest." It's a reminder to parents not to get stuck in that rut. Your children need to know that each of them will be held responsible for breaking the rules.

See Your Children with Fresh Eyes

If you "see" one of your children in every conflictual situation as "the one who always causes trouble," he will pick up on that and play the part. I once heard a saying: "A person can never grow from a hole." When a child is labeled negatively and is constantly being addressed as *that* child, he will live up to his title. Labeling your child is not only unfair to the child but it will backfire on you. Such a child will lose the will to try to improve his or her behavior. So, when you come to a situation involving that child, you need to use fresh eyes, eyes that aren't looking *at* them but *beyond* them at what they can be. Eyes that would be surprised to know that this child was at fault. Once you change your lenses, the child will see himself or herself differently as well and, over time, act differently. The child will no longer be held back by a label. When I see my child acting out consistently, I make sure to connect with him or her on a daily basis and stay away from assumptions and blame, especially when it comes to sibling rivalry. Instead I use phrases like, "Vivian would never use that language," "Frieda always shares," and "It can't be Eddy. He would never use his hands." When I *do* catch them doing the wrong things, I raise them up by saying, "That is very unlike you to behave that way. You are too special."

Communication Skills

"Ahhhhhhhh!"
"Wahhhhhhhh!"
"Shutuuuuppp!"
"Stooooppp!"
"You're soooo annoyinnnggg!"
"I hate youuuu!"
"I wish you were never born!"
"I'm gonna kill him!"

Sound familiar? Not very ideal ways of communicating our feelings, are they?

Healthy communication doesn't come naturally; it must be taught. Children need help to find the words to express their frustration. You can help them by validating their feelings, explaining how best to communicate them, and teaching them how to resolve conflict. "Honey, I see you're upset that Jack ate your last candy. Let's talk about how you can tell Jack that what he did isn't OK and what you can do in the future if he does it again." Practice role playing, and see how the scenario plays out.

Here are some examples of what healthy communication looks like.

> "Mom, Sam took my markers from my drawer and didn't ask me first."
> Mom: "I'm so glad you were able to communicate that to me in a calm voice. Now I can help resolve it."

> "Jason, you used my computer without asking me, and I have important schoolwork on it. I'd appreciate it if you ask me next time, so I can make sure my work is saved properly. Otherwise, I will need to put a password on it."

> "Jen, your clothes are all over the floor. Since we share a room, we need to be more considerate, so we don't annoy each other."

> "Lauren, you're wearing my top again. I explained to you last week that I don't want you wearing my clothes without asking me first. The next time it happens, I'm going to have to tell Mom and Dad."

This language may be foreign to some. Communication is a skill that takes time and patience to develop. In the beginning, you will need to "feed" these words to your children, so they can learn them. Once they know the language, they can rehearse and eventually adopt it. When you see your children use healthy communication skills, support them with positive reinforcement to reinforce the idea that calm and respectful language gets your attention and results in praise.

Problem-Solving Skills

There are several ways to teach the gift of problem-solving skills to children. The first step in any approach is to model how best to manage conflict: remain calm, communicate respectfully, validate, and use empathy. If you don't model these traits, it will be hard to teach your children because they inevitably learn from the example you set for them. Modeling healthy problem-solving skills will also create learning opportunities for your children in how to manage sibling rivalry.

Second, provide your kids with natural opportunities to learn. That means allowing sibling rivalry by not getting involved in every single conflict. This will give your kids the chance to start figuring out on their own how they communicate, what their triggers are, how to reflect on their character traits, and to experiment with ways to navigate conflict effectively.

Third, teach problem-solving skills by keeping an open dialogue about sibling conflict. For example:

- "Jake, I noticed you and Alan have been arguing a lot lately. Do you want to talk about what's going on?"
- "Alice, I noticed you and Elle are having trouble sharing the bathroom in the morning. Let's talk about it."

Encouraging dialogue shows you are present, nonjudgmental, and that you care. Communication will open a channel for you to teach.

You can also teach your children during a conflict by modeling and teaching at the same time, making it a "hands-on" learning experience. Here is a three-step approach to introduce problem-solving when addressing sibling rivalry.

1. Ask each child to calmly tell their side of the story.
2. Validate each child's feelings.
3. Ask each child for ideas on how to resolve the situation.

Here's an example of what the process looks like.

> Mom: "I see we're having a problem here. I want to hear both sides, so I can help you work this out. Eric, you first."
> (Isaac and Eric tell their side of the story.)
> Mom: "Eric, I can see that your feelings were hurt when Isaac took your microphone. Isaac, I can see you were angry that Eric was singing too loud, and that's why you grabbed the microphone from his hands. Now, how do you think we can resolve this?"
> Isaac: "He needs to be quiet when I ask him to stop singing."
> Eric: "No I don't. I don't have to listen to him."
> Mom: "Interesting. Eric, it *is* your choice not to listen to your brother when he asks you to stop singing, but I know you

are usually very considerate to your siblings when they are studying."

Eric: "But he yelled at me and grabbed my microphone."

Mommy: "I hear you, Eric. Isaac, Eric didn't respond well when you yelled at him. Do you think that if you used a calm voice, he would be more considerate?"

Isaac: "I doubt it."

Mommy: "Let's try to come up with a plan to avoid similar situations in the future, and then you can get back to your studies. Guys?"

Isaac: "I'll try not to yell next time."

Eric: "I'll try to be more considerate."

Mom: "That's an excellent plan."

In this scenario, the mother is the mediator. Her objective is to teach conflict resolution skills. By asking each child their side of the story, she sends the message that the situation will be judged objectively; the conflict will be seen with fresh eyes. After she hears both sides, she validates each child's feelings, which helps deflate the situation. Lastly, exploring solutions will help the children in terms of problem solving and compromise.

Keep in mind that it isn't helpful to debate who is right and who is wrong. There are no judges in the real world outside of the courtroom. The answer is usually subjective, and frankly, it doesn't matter. In fact, judgment will only cause more jealously and resentment, which will put you right back to square one of managing sibling rivalry. Training children to hear each other's side and act in a solution-oriented manner will help them grow up to be conscientious adults who use conflict-resolution skills with their peers and, ultimately, their spouse. Your children's spouses will thank you one day!

Special Sibling Activities

Providing fun activities for siblings to do together will create a positive bonding experience for them. Whether it's baking a cake for Grandma's birthday, cleaning your car with their water guns, or doing a Food Network cooking challenge together, these experiences will pave the way for a closer relationship in the future.

I heard a beautiful eulogy given by Rabbi Eli Mansour about a close friend of his who was a prominent member of the community, a business giant, and a wealthy man. As the story goes, Rabbi Mansour was invited to his friend's summer home. The rabbi explained that he assumed he would be pulling up to a mansion. Although the house was beautiful, it was small and modest considering this man's wealth. On the tour of the inside, the rabbi noticed there were only a few bedrooms, and the kids all shared rooms.

"Why don't the children have their own rooms?" Rabbi Mansour asked.

"I always want my kids to be close to each other," his friend replied. Keep in mind that this is a man who could have built whatever size house he wanted but chose to put his children in close proximity to each other. Would his life have been easier if everyone had their own space? Probably. Would he have had many more peaceful moments in the house? Definitely. But this man was looking toward the future and the connections he hoped his children would have throughout their lives.

When to Stay Out of It and When to Intervene

When it comes to sibling rivalry, it can be hard for parents to know when to intervene. As mentioned earlier, children sometimes need to be able to figure it out on their own. Here are some different, and escalating, levels of rivalry and suggestions for whether and how to get involved:

Normal bickering. If your children are arguing or fighting without physical or emotional harm, stay out of it. Getting involved in every altercation reduces the number of opportunities for your children to learn problem-solving skills, social skills, and coping skills. Children need the space to feel, communicate, and act, so they can rehearse these skills until they master them.

"Code orange" bickering. A little push, a bit of name calling, a little shouting. This is when you should step in, ask for both sides of the story, validate each child, and encourage them to come up with a solution that is fair to both. Remember: Stay neutral, calm, and collected.

World War III. There is no room for a positive learning experience from a natural consequence when it comes to flying furniture or the possibility of broken bones. If children engage in a physical altercation or are damaging each other emotionally, take the following steps:

1. Separate the children until they both calm down.
2. Hold a meeting about what happened.
3. Describe which rules were broken.
4. Validate each child's feelings.

5. Impose a consequence.
6. Follow up with a plan to avoid similar situations in the future. Prompting your children to come up with their own plan of action is the most effective way to avoid sibling rivalry.

What sort of consequences should you impose? Good question. As I explained in another section, I try to keep consequences as relatable and reasonable as possible. When dealing with a sibling rivalry, here are a few examples.

- If children disrupt family time, they lose out on family time at the next family outing. For example, children are fighting at the dinner table and, after multiple interventions, continue to be disruptive. After they are sent to their rooms, Mom and Dad call both children out to discuss the situation and impose a consequence. "It has been really unpleasant tonight for everyone in the house. We all should be able to come home to a peaceful family dinner. Since neither of you contributed to that, you won't be attending the Thursday night dinner outing with the family. We will miss having you with us, but we know you can do better and will make more of an effort to behave better in the future."
- If children are fighting over who has control over the remote for the TV, it gets turned off.
- If children are arguing over the computer, the computer is off limits.

Even when consequences are not directly relatable to the misbehavior, I try to create a connection when I present them to my children. For example, "Daddy and I feel it's best that you spend some time focusing on how you can improve your behavior. For that reason, your phones will be with us for a few days."

A Few More Tips on Intervention

A few issues frequently come up on the topic of sibling rivalry: time-outs, fighting over toys or electronics, and hitting.

Time-outs, "corner time," and separation time provide space for children to calm down and gain perspective. They also give parents time to regulate their emotions, so they can address the situation more effectively. It's essential to check in with your emotions and intentions when enforcing time-outs. This is the X-factor when it comes to discipline. If a parent's intent is to punish the child, get away from them, or put them down, time-outs are ineffective and unhealthy. However, when guided by love and purposeful intent, time-outs and separation are effective ways to teach children about inappropriate behaviors. When you send your child to a time-out, the child may essentially be calming down alone, but you don't want the child to feel isolated emotionally. You are simply teaching the child how to manage their feelings. When a parent is proactive (instead of reactive) in keeping their children's emotional needs at heart, the lesson will come through.

Time-outs or corner time are more effective when you remove the negative connotation that comes with those labels. Change the name to something more neutral and pleasant sounding like "cool-down spot," "calm-down time," or "refresh time." This will make it easier for your children to bounce back more quickly without feeling embarrassed or victimized.

Fighting over objects and hitting. When children are fighting over an object, remove it until both children can come up with a solution. As explained above, such an approach is beneficial because it allows you to address your children on a personal level without taking sides. It also encourages problem-solving skills.

When small children "use their hands," consider a time-out followed by a lesson: "Hitting is an unacceptable way to deal with a problem. Using words is the way to communicate when we are angry." For older children, separation is a must, whether it's taking a walk or going to their rooms. Once the children calm down, follow up with a conversation to discuss the situation further. Listen to their frustrations, validate their feelings (not their actions,) brainstorm ways to help them avoid using their hands in the future, and follow up with a consequence.

Don't force children to apologize. If they are too young to understand and process what they are saying, apologizing won't help. It may also encourage them to say a quick, meaningless "sorry" as a way to avoid a consequence. Instead, focus on having open and meaningful conversations about empathy and help them learn how to "feel" for others. Open their eyes to self-reflection, and explore ways they can avoid hurting someone's feelings in the future.

What if Yo Do All These Things, but Sibling Rivalry Remains Constant?

If sibling rivalry is constant, refer back to the list on page 79. Pay close attention to your children's feedback. If, for example, you keep hearing a consistent, "It's not fair; you never punish her," it's time to revisit the topics of "Favoritism" and "Making Each Child Feel Secure in Their Position in the Family." If you are hearing a consistent, "I'm not Esther! I don't like to play tennis on Sundays," revisit the topic of "Comparing." If you are hearing a consistent, "You always blame me!", revisit the topic of "Seeing children with fresh eyes." And remember, it takes time for children to learn these new skills before they can internalize and practice them, so be patient with yourself and your children.

Quotes to Hold On to

"Siblings are the people we practice on, the people who teach us about fairness and cooperation and kindness and caring- quite often the hard way."
—Dr. Pamela Dugdale

"A mother's love is whole, no matter how many times divided."
—Robert Brault (author)

"A sibling is the lens in which you see your childhood."
—Ann Hood (American novelist and short story writer)

7

Respect

You are not alone if the statements below are echoing through the walls of your home.

"Mom, you're so annoying!"

"Leave me alone, Dad!"

"Give me your Amazon password. I need a new bag for school."

"Mom, you owe me money."

"I need a ride to my friend's house NOW."

"You never . . .!"

R-E-S-P-E-C-T! I cannot help it; Aretha Franklin's song keeps ringing in my head.

If our great-grandparents heard the way our children speak to us, they would roll over in their graves. The current generation of kids does not have the same respect for adults that children had in previous times when the gap between the roles of parent and child was large. Parents were parents. Kids were kids. Teachers were teachers. Everyone was clear on their role. Over the years, this dynamic and these relationships have changed. In many ways, this generation of parents has come a long way when it comes to understanding children and meeting their emotional needs. We have so many resources to enhance our relationships with our children and give them the best possible care. At the same time, children now have louder voices. Their feelings are given more consideration, and they are treated more respectfully. Thumbs up to us! However, while we have stretched our patience and understanding, we have also stretched our boundaries when it comes to values and respect. Although times have changed, those values have remained consistent across the generations. We continue to rely on them as well as the moral codes of our past, what we stand for, the difference between right and wrong, and our principles.

When did the boundaries between parents and children become so blurry? Why are we so unsure of ourselves when implementing rules on respect and values? Simple. When we became more educated about parenting, we became more focused on hearing our children's voices, which are sometimes inconsistent with asserting ourselves as the authority. We now know all too well about the possible outcomes of "bad" parenting. We have become fearful of "damaging" our children by imposing our views onto them, so we tread lightly around discipline. The problem is, if we don't instill values and respect in our children, what kind of kids are we raising? Children aren't born knowing right from wrong. They don't pop out with a strong moral code. If you don't teach your children values and implement consequences when their actions go against those values, you will be raising your children to "grow" into uncivilized people who haven't internalized a sense of right and wrong. What does that look like?

- Children who do the wrong thing when no one is looking
- Children who are disrespectful to adults
- Children who spit their gum onto the street
- Children who don't say "Please" and "Thank you"
- Children who see someone who is hurt but walk past without helping
- Children who roll their eyes at the teacher
- Children who only care about themselves

When I was driving last week, I saw a young adult in the next car open his window and throw out his garbage at a red light: his coffee cup, gum wrappers, a banana peel, and even his dirty napkins. I don't know about anyone else, but if that were my child, I would be devastated. This "adult" wasn't thinking about anyone or anything but himself. Where did this person grow up? A zoo?

As I mentioned earlier, we didn't have many rules in our home when I was growing up. We could be hanging from the chandelier, and my mother wouldn't care. However, there was one rule we were all clear on: if we were moody or disrespectful, we were "dead." We would be sent to our rooms and the whole house would turn silent, as if someone had unplugged a loud stereo, and everyone stopped moving. We all knew that the punished child had crossed the line. Even though we were simply told to go to our rooms, it felt impactful because there were so few actions for which we were disciplined. We could eat, sleep, and play whenever and however we wanted, but when it came to respect and moody behavior, the music stopped, and the rules were enforced.

How do we raise our kids to be respectful of others? How do we avoid raising children like that one in the car next to me? The answer, again, is by modeling respect. Kids learn respect at home. Do you treat your children with kindness? Are you sincere and honest with them? How do you treat others? Do you greet people nicely on the street? Do you show respect to your spouse? Do you show respect to the elderly? As always, parenting starts with us—the parents. When it comes to disrespect, manners, or conduct, it's the same across the board. Modeling is the first step in teaching.

A mom once called me with concerns about her child using bad language. I asked if she ever used bad language. "Yes, sometimes," she replied. The night before, her kid even told her, "But you say those words too!" Rebuking bad language when a parent doesn't follow the same rule sends a mixed message. The child may be thinking, *I guess it can't be all that bad if Mommy and Daddy say these words. Maybe if I just do it a little or wait until I get older.*

Placing emphasis on respect at a young age is crucial for children to learn its importance as they grow up. As toddlers, when they ask for a cookie, teach them to say "Please." When they get the cookie, teach them to say, "Thank you." When an elderly person is leaving a store, hold the door open for them. It's our job, as parents, to teach our children respectful language and proper manners. What is more important than raising a good soul?

There is no room for "natural consequences" here. You cannot expect your children to learn to behave in line with your values without being deliberate and proactive. Yes, it's important to emphasize school responsibilities, hobbies, chores, and so on. But when it comes to the most important part of our job, creating good humans, we tend to become wishy-washy when disciplining disrespect. Part of the problem is that the word "respect" means different things to different people. The same goes for what is considered disrespectful. The solution is being clear on the values *you* find important that don't require the approval of others. How many times have you heard comments like the following? "Seriously, you won't allow him to go to the party?" "You're stuck in a time warp." "That's not realistic." "Ah, she's just a kid!" Want to hear my answer? "It's my kid, and she's going to turn into an adult one day. Are you going to take responsibility for her actions? No. I am. Thanks for the advice but no thanks."

Tips on Addressing Disrespectful Behavior

When children act and speak with disrespect, it creates a powerful emotional trigger and can be particularly challenging for parents to deal with it. Here are a few tips on how to address disrespectful behavior.

Stay calm and collected. Children often use disrespect to trigger a parent or get attention. Don't get emotionally hooked when a child speaks disrespectfully to you. Feeding that behavior with a reaction, especially a negative one, may encourage more of the same. Remaining calm, cool, and collected models respectful behavior while showing children that their behavior will not lead to the results they want. Replace being reactive with a steady, intentional response.

Make sure there is no miscommunication. Did your child ignore you or not hear you? Did the child use bad language, or did you mishear her? Is the child whining or acting intentionally disrespectful? Sometimes children don't have the skills to successfully communicate their needs, so they whine. It's not personal or disrespectful; they just don't know how to speak in a way that others can hear and understand them. Encourage them to say it again using another tone.

Identify where the behavior is coming from. Even though it is unacceptable under any circumstance to be disrespectful, you need to know the root of what the child is saying. Does the child feel hurt or angry at you? Why? Is it a matter of teaching self-control or something a little deeper, like the child calling out for love and attention? If a child is consistently acting out, address the disrespect right away. However, it's just as important—if not more so—to balance the consequence with a positive connection. Suggesting some alone time to talk and connect goes a long way when it comes to building trust.

Separate the child from the disrespectful behavior. Saying things like "*You* are disrespectful," "*You* need to learn self-control," or "*You* have anger issues" is too personal and can damage a child's self-image. Instead, try using language like this: "I see you are angry, but that language is unacceptable. In this house, the rule is that we never speak to an adult that way." By labeling the behavior and not the child, you steer away from damaging their self-esteem. Although it may be uncomfortable for you to validate your children's feelings when they act disrespectfully, remember that you aren't validating their behavior; you are validating their feelings. This will create more opportunities for teaching a better way to express themselves.

Consequences for disrespect. The most logical and relatable consequence for disrespect is separation. When a child isn't considerate of others or other people's feelings, the logical consequence is time away. Whether it's room time or a time-out, separation is an effective form of discipline when it comes to disrespect.

- *The timing of consequences.* When it comes to disrespect, I recommend acting quickly with the consequence. That doesn't mean being reactive or impulsive. You can still be cool, calm, and collected while acting swiftly. The message, then, becomes clear: there is no tolerance for disrespect in your home. You can discuss the issue later, but in the moment, it's time for separation.
- *Discussion.* After implementing a consequence, the next step is an open discussion on the topic. Some children will be ready as soon as they finish the separation. For others, it may be too soon because they need more time to cool down. Only you can decide the best timing for the follow-up conversation.

Accept the child's apology, and try not to hold a grudge. True apologies look like this:

- "I'm sorry for the way I spoke to you earlier. I was just very angry at Joseph."
- "I will try not to talk like that again."

It can take a lot for any of us to apologize, but it's especially hard for children to self-reflect, take responsibility, and admit wrongdoing. Take this time to highlight their willingness to admit fault as an admirable quality. Demonstrating unconditional love and forgiveness when there are disruptions in your relationship will go a long way to protecting and building your connection going forward.

Values

My mother jokes about how my younger brother was the most mischievous child on the planet, but whenever he saw a neighbor coming home with packages, he was the first to run outside and help her bring them in. This was not as coincidental as my mother thought. My brother, like the rest of us, was taught that staying true to our values—not his grades, athleticism, or his accomplishments, but seeing and respecting the people around him—is most important. My parents taught me the importance of values, and even now, when an older person is walking toward me on the street, I can feel my father's hands pulling me aside to let them pass, just as I take my own children's hands to do the same. I bet all of my siblings will tell you the same thing.

You also pass your values on to your children by involving them in the things *you* value. By giving them a role in holiday planning, charity events, sick visits, birthday cards, and so on, you instill tour values in them. Infusing your values takes effort, positive reinforcement, prompting, and creativity. When you see your children start to independently weave your values into their personalities, it's a truly rewarding experience. Here are a few examples of using positive strategies for teaching children your values.

- "Did you see the way that man spoke to the waiter? I can see how uncomfortable that made you feel. I felt the same way. In our family, that kind of talk is not in line with our values."
- "Cousin Emily is coming over for dinner. Can you help me count the seats and see if we need another chair? [Which he does.] I think you are right! We are one chair short. You are really considerate for counting the seats. Making sure our guests are comfortable is an important value of the Gindi family, and I can see you share that same value!"
- "When your brother scraped his knee and was really hurting, you ran to get him a Band-Aid. I noticed that you are always the first one there to help someone when they fall down. That is a truly special value you have."
- "Zac, Grandma told me you called her when she was sick with the flu. Taking the time to make someone happy when they are struggling is an important value of our family. You should be really proud of yourself!"

When I think about my grandparents, I laugh at their funny rules and weird pet peeves, but I also realize that the things that make me laugh are a narrative of their values and reflect their "book of life." Each time I put on a black dress, I think of my Grandmother Norma A'H and how much she disapproved when anyone in the family wore black clothing. In her eyes, it represented the clothes of people in mourning. It was an important value to her. She wore bright pink lipstick to show how she celebrated life. I do like black clothing, but I also celebrate the value of life—passed on by my grandmother—by putting on pink lipstick whenever I wear black.

Roots

Strong roots are the anchors of a family. Who you are, where you come from, your culture, family values, the importance of your heritage, and a commitment to a bigger purpose are the ingredients of a strong home. In our home, it's Judaism. In others, it will be something else. Sometimes life deals you a tough hand and forces you to pause and reflect to find your center. That's when the value of your roots come in. The comforting memories that connect you to who you are become your anchor when life gets hard. Your deeply embedded roots provide a familiar comfort and a feeling of security that becomes a padding for your fall. It's the safe place to come back to. That "home" is where your journey began, and sometimes by revisiting those steps, you gain a fresh perspective that helps you persevere through the challenges. As a parent, your job is to keep watering these roots. In our home, sticking together, putting family needs before social obligations, family dinners, meaningful holiday experiences with extended family, giving back to the community, lighting Shabbat candles with our daughters, going to Shul with our sons, and our many inside jokes (and dysfunctions) give our family its unique character and make life a little easier to laugh through. Our family's identity becomes our children's anchor that steadies them through the ups and downs.

When I look back at my childhood, I don't remember all that much other than simple moments and experiences. Long, boring holiday nights with cousins and family. Walking to the corner to rent a movie with my siblings. Watching my father pay the bills on Sunday mornings with his calculator and highlighter. Coffee time with my grandmother. Waiting for the bus to take me to camp while I rocked on Grandpa Jack's chair. The scent of the fresh dollar bill my Great Grandma Serena gave us whenever we visited. The awesome sleepovers on our broken pull-out couch. The rough rides down the staircase in a sleeping bag at my cousin's house. Bunking out with ten kids during our motel stays on family vacations. As I got older, I realized how the simplest of moments had the most impact on me as an adult because they weren't just moments; they became my anchor. I hope that is also true for you.

Quotes to Hold On To

"Kids do not remember what you try to teach them. They remember what you are."
—Jim Henson (American puppeteer, animator, and cartoonist, best known as the creator of *The Muppets*)

"When roots are deep, there is no reason to fear the wind."
—Lori Bregman (Life coach, author, and doula)

"Enjoy the little things in life, because one day you will look back and realize they were the big things."
—Kurt Vonnegut (author)

8

The Apprehensive Disciplinarian

After all the talk of discipline, respect, and consequences, a certain group of parents still need some extra support in this area. This chapter pertains to you if:

- You always feel unsure of your parenting approach
- You shy away from discipline
- You constantly feel defeated
- You are emotionally drained and exhausted from doubt
- You don't feel secure in your position as a mom or dad
- You lack the courage to set limits
- You fear confrontation
- You constantly feel guilty

This chapter will be less pertinent (though still worth a review) if:

- You gravitate toward discipline
- You rarely feel guilty for disciplining
- You are neutral to confrontation
- Your children feel a level of fear when they break a rule

Do you ever feel like you are being punched in the stomach whenever you muster the courage to face confrontation? Are all the feelings you have about discipline tangled up in threads that run so deep that you don't even know where they began? Have you lost your inner strength to keep trying?

I have been there. It's painful. But is it ever too late to change? Absolutely not.

Many of us are born without aggressive traits. We simply don't like to argue or fight. In fact, we dislike belligerent people who flare their tempers. Though these character traits work well in many ways, when it comes to parenting, sometimes we wish we could snap our fingers and turn into someone else—someone like an army general! The good news is that when it comes to parenting, there is room for different styles. While a less domineering parenting style leads to a more approachable parent, which is helpful for connection, a more authoritative personality leads to a more structured and managed home. The perfect balance lies in being able to parent with both warmth and control based on the situation.

For many parents, it isn't easy to set limits, establish rules, and follow through on them. Why? For the same reason other parents have a hard time adjusting the rules and being more flexible; it is just a difference in personality and parenting style. Pioneering psychologist Diana Baumrind proposes three main parenting styles.

- Authoritarian: Parents set strict rules and follow through with harsh punishments. This style is associated with children who have lower social skills and reduced self-esteem.
- Permissive: Parents set few rules and enforce few or no punishments. They have no demands or expectations and are not responsive to their children's needs. This is associated with children who have higher aggression and lower maturity.
- Authoritative: This is the middle ground between the two parenting styles above. Parents set rules and enforce them. They are demanding but responsive to their children's needs by having open discussions with them. Here, children have the possibility of compromise. Although parents have the final say, the children are involved. This parenting style is associated with children who are self-reliant, socially competent, and have higher self-esteem.

Every home and family is different, each with its own challenges and difficulties. Even authoritative parents may have difficulty managing a specific child—for example, one who is more defiant or persistent. A child's behavior can affect a parent's style as well. By keeping an open mind and setting reasonable expectations, the next few tips will help you reach that middle ground where parents set rules, enforce them, and leave room for discussion and compromise.

But first, it's important to get some clarity on the "boss" child who seems to want or even prefer the title. Whether or not they are willing to admit it, children want and yearn for security and limits; they want parents. Deep down, they need to feel safe and nurtured and know the benefits of boundaries and structure. To get that, they need the security of parental authority.

The key to establishing and/or regaining authority is to start small. Choose one area you want to work on, and focus on that. And know that it won't happen overnight. You will need time, patience, and a measure of inner strength—a strength you may yet have to discover.

Tips on Establishing Authority in Your Home

When a home has been running a certain way for a long time, it can be especially challenging to pivot in a different direction. The following tips serve as a guide for your next steps forward.

Discussing the "new authority." Here is some possible language: "Hi, my name is Mom, and this is Dad. We want to inform you that things are going to change around here and that we will be taking back the title of 'parents.' Just to be clear, you won't be getting it back until you are married and no longer living under this roof. This is how things are going to go moving forward. Thank you for your time, my sweet little Janet." Put the gist of this in your own words!

Implement clear rules and clear consequences. Don't do this in a mean or punitive way but in a way that firmly establishes your authority. Rules and consequences need to be crystal clear in advance. Start with one new rule, and discuss it during a family meeting. For example: Mom and Dad decide they are going to implement a "no disrespect" rule. During the family meeting, they discuss what behavior and words qualify as disrespect and state the consequences that will be enforced if the children don't follow the rule. "In our family, there will be no tolerance for disrespect. From now on, when someone speaks disrespectfully, they will be separated and placed in their rooms. There will be no discussion or argument. After you have spent time in your room, we will come to discuss the issue further with you."

Keep each situation independent from the others. Don't get "tangled up in blue," as Bob Dylan says. Stay present, and act with intent. Do not look forward or backward. Stay in the moment. For example, avoid the following: "She *always* speaks to me with disrespect." "He is *going to* hate me if I keep punishing him."

Talk less, and act quickly. Repeat the rule and consequence in as few words as possible: "We never speak with disrespect. It is room time." Then act swiftly. Don't worry if they say things like "Buuuut Maaaa, you never listen to me. I only said that because . . ." or "I did not know that was a bad word." Follow through, and remain cool, calm, and collected.

Stay neutral. Don't get triggered by personal attacks or guilt. Keep moving forward. Pretend you are walking on the beach. You aren't angry, mad, upset, or happy, just neutral, calm, and unbothered.

Stay consistent, and follow through. There are no exceptions when it comes to following through. Rules are rules. No ifs, ands, or buts. Children who are used to being the boss will not react pleasantly or obediently when it comes to giving up their title. Keep this in mind when you follow through. Establishing your authority will feel threatening at first, and bossy children will probably assert themselves even more than they did before you stepped up. Don't be discouraged, and don't allow yourself to be manipulated. Stay focused. Do not doubt yourself. It will get easier.

Don't be afraid of your children's reaction when setting new boundaries. It can be really hard to see your children upset and angry, but that doesn't mean you are doing it wrong. Set boundaries based on what you think is right, not what you think your children will swallow. The latter will only allow room for manipulation and guilt. Stay confident in your right to parent and your ability to handle your children through tantrums, fights, and arguments. Don't succumb to self-doubt and guilt. Remember your healthy affirmations.

- "I am a good parent."
- "Just because my child isn't happy right now doesn't mean I'm a bad parent."
- "I am doing the right thing. Period."
- "This is going to get better."

Embrace your role. Get comfortable in your position. There is no such thing as a perfect parent; we all make mistakes. Sometimes you will get it wrong, and it's OK.

Parent with warmth and control. Discipline doesn't have to be negative or cold. It can—and should—be warm and loving. If your intention is to teach your children what inappropriate behavior looks like and that certain behaviors are unacceptable, you are actually demonstrating love. Pat yourself on the back for your efforts!

Quotes to Hold On To

"There is no such thing as being a perfect parent, so just be a real one."
—Sue Atkins (Television presenter and author known for her work in parenting)

"How can you expect your children to meet expectations when you set no boundaries?"
—Jo Frost (English television personality, nanny, and author)

"The difference between punishment and discipline is a powerful child."
—Danny Silk (author and speaker)

9

Teens

Parents of adolescents know that this topic deserves an entire chapter, even a book. The topic of adolescence keeps my phone ringing.

- "She has an attitude problem."
- "She is constantly rolling her eyes at me and jetting to her room after school."
- "He doesn't talk to me anymore."
- "He always wants us to leave him alone."
- "The constant arguing is killing our relationship."
- "She hates me."

Does any of this sound familiar? Although all children are unique, acting out is typical of adolescence. Getting some insight into what children are feeling during these turbulent years is important.

Adolescence is a time for establishing oneself as an individual, for exploring independence. Teens are exercising their right to use their voices, and they yearn to feel heard and respected. Although they aren't yet adults, they would like to be treated as such. At the same time, they want to avoid responsibilities and act like toddlers. In short, they want it both ways. It's the normal pattern of growing up. By understanding the typical adolescent profile, we can begin to parent them more effectively.

Behaviors that fit the adolescent profile include the following:

- Verbal aggression
- Frustration
- Impulsivity
- Changing moods
- Argumentativeness
- Selfishness
- Defiance
- Narcissism
- Irresponsibility
- Insecurity
- Persistence
- The need for privacy
- Fatigue
- Constant hunger

It may sound like the profile of a serial killer, but do not panic! This is when children are transitioning from dependence to independence, and that's a huge thing. They need to undergo the painful but liberating process of separating from their parents to become their own people. There is no "cure" for adolescence. We don't have the power to control our teenagers' behavior, and we wouldn't want to because it would stunt their growth. But there are ways to navigate adolescence by changing how you approach it to allow for an easier transition and a more peaceful home.

Riding the Currents of Adolescence

When it comes to parenting a teen, you need to adjust and prioritize. Here are a few points that can serve as a foundation.

Build a connection. The only tool you can rely on at this stage is your connection with your kids. (Refer back to "The Vitamins" on p. 47 to learn the skills of building a connection with your child.) Keep an open dialogue, and refrain from passing judgment. With adolescents, gentle guidance is a must if you want to maintain a strong relationship. Focus on understanding them instead of directing them. Although at times you may feel that your influence is nonexistent, you have a more significant role than you realize. Parents often tell me that it's hard to find the time to connect with their teens because they are on different schedules. Having family meals together is a good option for catching up and connecting. Other ideas include exercising together, cooking together, and shopping together.

Choose your battles. Giving in on the things that don't go against your primary values or principles is key. Many times, adolescents don't care about what they're asking for, but they battle it out anyway. Why is that?

- They are demonstrating their right to exercise their voice.
- They are exploring their positions and developing their identities.
- They want to feel respected.
- They want the freedom to make their own decisions and choices.
- They are figuring out how to have their needs met.

A mother once called me because she was concerned that her teenage son was demanding coffee in the mornings. She told him that coffee isn't healthy for a growing child. That night he came home with a Starbucks cup in his hand. I listened as the mother shared all of the other issues she is having with her son. I noticed a pattern: They kept getting into it over relatively minor things. You may disagree, but I told the mom to buy a coffee machine. "But coffee is unhealthy for a teenager," you may say. Yes, it is, but in this case I felt it was best for the mom to work on her relationship with her son rather than exert her control in an area that wasn't especially important. By showing up with a Starbucks, the boy was exercising his right to make his own choices. Letting him drink coffee would take that battle out of the relationship and make it a non-issue. Keeping this is mind, the mom was able to let go a little.

There are two important points here. First, allow your children, especially teens, to make decisions. Second, by not interfering in the small choices, natural consequences will hopefully guide them to make the right choices. Getting involved in every decision may lead to power struggles, which is what this mom was struggling with. So, choose your battles. It will give your teen a chance to learn decision making while minimizing family conflict. More importantly, when intervention *is* necessary, it will be more impactful.

Again, it's important to note that all children are different. Some teens will accept a "no" without an argument; others will exert their control wherever they can. In the end, "mom knows best." Just be conscious of your child's feedback and adjust accordingly.

Focus on being heard, not winning. If you want to stop the arguing, stop asserting your point of view through power/control during the teenage years. Adolescent children are yearning to be heard and to feel understood, so if you assert yourself too forcefully, it will only lead to a power struggle, and they will wear you down until you cannot see straight. It takes two tango, so get off that dance floor!

What does "not winning but being heard" look like? Back to the coffee example. Instead of forbidding your teen from having coffee, acknowledge his or her desire, and share your concerns. After that, allow the teen to make the choice.

What about situations when you *need* to win? What if your teen refuses to listen to you when the issue really is significant? Good question. Remember, you can't control whether or not your kids listen to you, but you can control the consequence when they don't follow the rules. Of course, you need to communicate these consequences clearly *before* an incident; otherwise, you will be creating an atmosphere of unfairness and resentment. Once teens can predict the consequences of their actions, they will be less likely to break the rules. If they do break them, it's important to follow through on those consequences. If your teens constantly break the rules, try the following.

1. Make sure there aren't too many rules in place that hinder independence.
2. Revisit the section in the discipline chapter on "logical consequences" to make sure your rules fall in line with the three Rs: reasonable, relatable, and respectful.
3. Confirm that you are consistently following through on consequences. If not, it may not be clear to the teen that his or her misbehavior will result in a consequence.

Avoid ultimatums that push you and your teen into a corner, and be crystal clear on the rules from the outset.

Giving them space to make choices. Adolescents want to come up with their own solutions. They need to feel capable and successful of running their lives in order for them to develop healthy self-esteem. The more space you give them when it comes to making smaller choices, the more space is left for your involvement in the bigger ones. You need to be savvy about navigating your involvement. I like to ask my daughter what her choices are and how she thinks each one will turn out. By encouraging her to explore options out loud, I allow her to see them more clearly, and, more importantly, I get a chance to express my own ideas about possible outcomes.

Create an atmosphere of trust. Telling the truth can be scary for kids who have broken the rules, but it's important that your children feel comfortable telling you they made a poor choice. Adolescence involves navigating some difficult decisions. When you keep an open line of communication with your teens, you can share your input and support better decision making. We all want our kids to be honest with us about drugs, alcohol, smoking, intimacy, and other delicate topics. It's especially important to emphasize that no matter what your teens do, you will never **be angry with them. Removing that fear can save a child's life.**

Reward responsible behavior with more independence. Highlighting smart behavior will likely lead to even more conscientious behavior. Positive reinforcement is a must. "Jay, I noticed you came home at 10 o' clock last night like we asked you too. We are really proud of how responsible you are. Feel free to go out next Saturday night as well."

Acceptance. Accept your children for who they are, and love them unconditionally. Be proud of them just for being themselves. Focus on *their* dreams and goals, not yours. Acceptance will allow you to support your teens on their own path through life and will prevent many unnecessary battles before they start.

Encourage productivity. Keep them busy! Teens have a lot of energy, and they need to exert it. They also need opportunities to feel successful and accomplished. Whether it's chores that require physical movement, a part-time job, or running a few household errands, encourage your teens to be contributing members of your home and society. This is not quite as easy as it sounds. You will need your wits about you to keep coming up with creative ways of channeling your teen's energy into productivity. Take some time to think of ways to motivate them until it becomes habitual.

For example, Dad decides he wants to start mowing his own lawn. He asks his son, Zac, to go to Home Depot with him and help pick out a new mower. Then he asks Zac if he can help mow the lawn once a week, telling him that since lawn mowing costs thirty dollars a month, he is happy to pay Zac the same for his help. Zac needs some extra cash and takes the job.

For parents, the emotional roller-coaster ride of adolescence can be challenging, but it can also be rewarding. From infancy through adulthood, we raise our children through every stage of life. Watching our hard work and dedication come to fruition is special. Take a moment to applaud yourself for the sacrifices you have made and the physical and emotional work you have put in to get your teen to this point. It is truly an accomplishment! Your baby has now reached the threshold of independence. Somehow, it all becomes worth it. And if it doesn't feel like it's been worth it yet, be patient. It will be.

More than likely, your children will never understand all you have done for them until they have their own children. You can tell them until you are blue in the face, but until they experience parenthood themselves, you will never get the thank-you that you feel you deserve. As a teenager, I thought my parents were dinosaurs who didn't know anything about anything. I walked through my adolescent years with my eyes rolled back. It's funny how things change when you become a parent. Even now, I call my mother and ask for her advice on raising my children. I also ask her how the heck she managed with us for all those years while keeping a smile on her face. Although a little late, I thank my parents for all the sacrifices they made for me and my siblings. I am waiting for the day I get that phone call from my own kids, and I will make sure they know exactly what they put us through! My Grandma Norma (A"H—the Hebrew for someone who has passed away) used to say that my brother, Eddie, was "payback" for all that my father put her through while growing up. I know she is laughing up in heaven . . .

Quotes to Hold On To

"A butterfly has to break out of its cocoon and a bear has to tear and claw its way out of the shell. They don't get to the next stage of their lives passively. And unfortunately, neither do adolescents."
—James Lehman (child behavioral therapist, co-creator of the Total Transformation program)

"You are the single greatest influence in your children's lives, even in the know-it-all teen years."
—Leah DeCesare (author of *Naked Parenting: 7 Keys to Raising Kids with Confidence*)

"I know what I want, I have a goal, an opinion . . . Let me be myself and then I am satisfied. I know that I'm a woman, a woman with inward strength and plenty of courage."
—Anne Frank (German-Dutch diarist of Jewish origin best known for *The Diary of a Young Girl*)
"Our kids might not be little anymore, but the toddler in them lies just below the surface."
—From the website Raising Teens Today

PART III: THE OUTSIDE WORLD

10

Social Connections

We raise our children with the unconditional love and acceptance they deserve. When they go out into the real world and come home from school one day with a sad face, we know the inevitable has happened: they have come to the harsh realization that not everyone accepts them for who they are. I can still name the kids who taught each of my children that lesson. It hurts.

Social goals are tricky. On one hand, you want your children to feel socially accepted. On the other hand, you don't want them to think they need to change for others to like or accept them. The question to reflect on is, "What is *my* role as a parent when it comes to social goals, and how can I help my children build social connections without compromising who they are?" There is a fine line between building social connections and being true to yourself. Teaching this distinction can be challenging.

Let's start with what we already know. For example, self-esteem is acquired through knowing your worth and accepting yourself uncon-ditionally. We also know that imposing social goals onto our kids isn't parenting in their best interest. Internalize that for a moment. Social baggage is real. Whether you grew up socially popular or struggled to feel accepted, you can't parent your kids with the intent that they follow in your footsteps. You also shouldn't shield them from the pain you went through. Both approaches have a common theme: you. Remember that your children are not an extension of you but individual souls. So, throw your social expectations out the window, and focus on your children's individual needs.

As for social connections, they are an important part of living a satisfying life. Studies show that positive social connections contribute to health, longevity, and overall happiness. People need people. We need to feel understood by and connected to others. In short, your kids will benefit tremendously by having good friends and feeling connected.

So, how do you raise your kids to become socially well-adjusted without compromising who they are as people? By raising them with healthy self-esteem and giving them the tools to become socially comfortable. That doesn't mean transforming your kids into Mr. and Ms. Popular or "making them" get over their shyness or become more reserved. It's about accepting your children's personalities as they are and then supporting them on their journey by teaching them the skills they need to connect with others.

Teaching Appropriate Social Skills

Social skills help children interact effectively with others. They include knowing when and how to use manners, asking for permission before acting, thinking before speaking, and sharing, listening, and compromising, among others. These skills are also important for building connections. Similar to "communication skills," there are several ways to teach social skills.

Modeling. If you want your kids to learn appropriate social skills, you need to model what they look like. The way you treat guests, the way you greet people, the way you communicate when we're upset, the way you cope in uncomfortable situations, the care you show for friends—all of these can be examples of the right way to interact with people. When your kids hear you on the phone talking about a "stupid friend" or saying "I shouldn't tell you this about her but . . ." they pick up on it. They will mimic this behavior, and it will have a negative impact on their social lives. If, on the other hand, you model healthy conduct, you are raising the bar and teaching them how to initiate and maintain positive social relationships.

Manners. Some behaviors need to be taught directly, such as "manner words." A mom I speak with has such words pasted on the wall: "Please." "Thank you." "May I . . ." "I would prefer . . ." "Hello." "Would you like . . ." And so on. Whenever her kids use a manner word, they get a star on their chart. I love this idea! When my kids were younger, and we went out for dinner, we would play "the manners game" while waiting to order. I would give them examples of scenarios in which people were or weren't using their manners. They would have to say if that person's actions were appropriate or inappropriate. I would make it fun: "A child eats with his hands." "A mom licks her fingers." "A dad swings his fork in the air." "A child puts a napkin on his lap before he eats." It was a great opportunity to teach social etiquette.

Communication skills. Helping your children learn to use healthy language and think before they speak can be taught through everyday experiences as well as role playing. Role playing is a lot of fun. For example, you can pretend to be a "difficult child" and see how your children reacts to the behavior. "No, it's mine!" you call out. Your children will probably laugh, but it will also prompt them to respond properly during their next play date. Refer to the chapter on sibling rivalry for more on communication skills.

Sharing. The gift of giving and sharing can be taught at an early age. Use positive reinforcement (like praise), and encourage generosity by reading books about sharing. Once again, role playing is another great way to teach children how to share. Prompt your children before a play-date by sitting down with them for a "pre-playdate." For example, if your children are at an age where they are afraid their playdates will "steal" their toys when they share them, reassure them that their toys will stay at home with them when their playdates leave. Praise their efforts when they show a spirit of sharing, and validate their feelings when they are uncomfortable. Confirm that the toys are still there. For older children, plant the seed about how givers always gain more than receivers and that giving to others will make them happy.

Being a good listener. Children learn how to listen by being listened to, so model that behavior by listening when your children speak to you. Children also learn to be good listeners by practicing. Highlight when your children are using their "listening" ears, and teach the importance of being heard and understood.

- "Wow, I noticed you listened to your brother when he told you about feeling left out by his friends. You are a great and caring listener."

- "When Jake asked you to stop singing, you really heard him."

Being respectful of others. Respect starts at home. You can teach the value of respect by modeling it and implementing rules on disrespect. Refer to the chapter on respect for more insights on this.

Having a positive attitude. My mother described our behavior as "sucky" whenever we were nagging, complaining, or generally unpleasant to be around. We weren't allowed to be sucky. If we were, we had to go to our rooms until our attitude changed. So, ban sucky behavior, and model (there's that word again!) a positive attitude. Positive behavior is contagious, like when someone starts laughing, and you can't help but smile. You can also teach your children some healthy affirmations and how to see the positive in every situation. For example, "Today is going to be a great day" or "I know it's raining, but now we can finish that project you started yesterday!" (You can read more about helping your kids acquire a positive attitude in the next chapter.)

Patience. Always helpful when in social situations, patience is taught through practice. A great way to teach children patience is to use positive reinforcement when they are already waiting for something, such as their turn in a game or standing in line for ice cream. "You are waiting so patiently." "Wow! This game was so fun to play as a family. Everyone waited patiently for their turn!" Some books that promote patience include *Llama Llama Red Pajama* by Anna Dewdney, *Betty the Bunny Loves Chocolate Cake* by Michael B. Kaplan, and *The Berenstain Bears: Patience, Please* by Mike Berenstain.

Good sportsmanship. Playing games at home can be very helpful by providing a hands-on learning experience. Whether you win or lose, you can highlight the joy in playing games and spending time together. Still, it will take time for some children to learn that winning is not the goal. Remain patient, and validate their feelings when they have a hard time losing. Prompting your child on possible outcomes before a competition or game is a good idea: "Honey, playing sports can be really competitive. As you know, only one team can win today, and that may be hard to swallow. Let's talk about it." Some books that promote sportsmanship include *Cheetah Can't Lose* by Bob Shea, *Pete the Cat: Play Ball!* by James Dean, *Number One Sam* by Greg Pizzoli, *Don't Throw It to Mo!* by David A. Adler, and *Winners Never Quit* by Mia Hamm.

Flexibility. Teaching children from an early age to accept a "no" and to shift their attitude when they don't get their way is another helpful skill for their social toolbox. There is a fine line between knowing when to hold your ground and when to be flexible, and some children have trouble giving in on, well, everything. These kids need to stretch their flexibility to maintain good relationships. In Judaism, being flexible is called being *mavatar*. When a person is *mavatar*, they give in for the sake of peace. It takes a lot of strength to be able to give in. You will hear me say, "Who's going to be mavatar?" at least once a day in my home. It highlights the character strength of flexibility. I also use positive rein-forcement when a child does accept a "no" or gives in easily when called for or when appropriate. For example, when my children hop into the car, there is always an argument over seating arrangements. If one of them gives in and says, "Fine, you can sit here," I jump right in. "Look how flexible you are! Because of you, the car ride will be more pleasant for the whole family."

Preserving Self-Esteem When Faced with Negative Social Experiences

Children with healthy self-esteem are less likely to seek approval and acceptance from others than children with low self-esteem. So, it's espe-cially important to teach them from an early age that not everyone will love and accept them—and that it's perfectly OK. It may still be difficult to experience, but when someone rejects them, simply reassure them that it's the other child's loss, not theirs. The last thing you want your children to feel is a need to be liked or accepted in order to feel good about them-selves. That insecurity will make them vulnerable to peer pressure.

How you respond to your children's negative social experiences can make or break their self-esteem. Here are some examples of how not to respond.

- "Well, were you nice to him?"
- "Did you act bossy when you were at his house?"
- "Maybe if you practice playing sports, you'll fit in better."
- "She probably didn't invite you because you weren't very nice to her last week."

Even if your child does act bossy sometimes or you know their in-teractions will improve if they change their behavior, it isn't helpful to blame them. Better to learn the areas in which you would like to see them improve and slowly work on these. Otherwise, the message you are sending is, "It's *your* fault they don't like you." Once that message is internalized, a child may go through life thinking there is something wrong with him or her. My Grandma Foozy likes to say, "If they do not see you, it is their loss! Period."

Exposing your children to different groups of friends will allow them to choose the ones who make them feel most comfortable and valuable. Friends should make us feel good. When a "friend" persistently makes a child feel bad about himself or herself, that person is not a friend worth having, and it's time to find someone else. Although you cannot control your children's experiences, you can do your best to place them in environments that give them opportunities to feel good about themselves. Most importantly, you need to connect with your children, so they feel comfortable enough to come to you when faced with difficulties and rejection.

Unfortunately, some parents add to their children's social pressure because they so desperately want them to fit in. They say things like, "Honey, you should call Jason and see what the boys are up to today. You aren't staying home today." "Did you call Sharon back? Her mom told me she's having a party in a few weeks, and I know you won't want to miss it." When you pressure children like this, they might respond by trying to please you and spend time with kids who don't make them feel good. Or they might hang out with the wrong crowd. When you add to your children's social pressures, you also close the doors for communication and support because you introduce judgement, however well-meaning your intentions.

Parents can alleviate much of the social pressures their children experience by keeping an open dialogue, spending quality time with them without judgment, and supporting them regardless of their social success. Make your home a safe space for your kids to be themselves. They need to feel that their social life doesn't affect you personally. Create a distance between your desires for your children's social success and what is natural for them. Whether they have a million friends or one, it shouldn't matter. Social success is not a measure of their worth—not for them and not for you. When your children know that, they will more likely seek friends who value them for who they are.

Bullying

When someone intentionally and repeatedly causes harm to another person, parents need to get involved. Bullying comes in four forms: physical, verbal, social exclusion, and cyber (online).

- **Physical bullying:** When a child hits, kicks, pushes, threatens,

116

steals, harasses, humiliates, or ruins another's belongings.

- **Verbal bullying:** Teasing, taunting, cursing, or name calling.
- **Social exclusion:** When someone spreads rumors, lies, threatens to exclude, or pressures a child to do something they aren't comfortable with.
- **Cyberbullying:** Using technology to harass, humiliate, taunt, threaten, spread lies or rumors, or verbally abuse a person. Cyber bullies aren't confined to a setting. They hide behind a computer screen without having to identify themselves.

How to help your child if he/ she is bullying or falls victim to a bully:

- Talk to your child about bullying. Proactively discuss what bullying is and how to prevent it.
- Encourage the importance of reaching out if they experience any type of bullying.
- Seek professional help.
- Get support. No child should ever have to experience the effects of bullying, and my heart goes out to those who do.

Quotes to Hold On To

"If I am not for myself, who will be for me? And being only for myself, what am I?"
—Rabbi Hillel the Elder (Jewish religious leader, sage, and scholar) Pirkei Avot 1:14

"Why fit in when you were born to stand out?"
—Dr. Seuss (Theodor Seuss Geisel, an American children's book author, political cartoonist, illustrator, poet, animator, screenwriter, and filmmaker)

"Alone, we can do so little. Together, we can do so much."
—Helen Keller

11

The Sucky One

A mother called me recently to talk about a child who has been act-ing "sucky" for a while. She explained that her daughter is always moping around and that when she does speak, it's in a "naggy" voice. I've known this mom for a while now, and I know she can be a little sucky herself. I asked how her own mood had been lately. "Regular," she replied. I suggested that she put on music when her kids come home and ignore the routine responsibilities for an hour. It worked! The kids start-ed laughing and singing. A few days later, I said, "Now, do it on Sunday morning." She couldn't believe what a difference the music made in the house. Then I connected the dots for her. In short, a positive attitude is contagious. Although it's great to refrain from yelling or acting out of anger, it's not enough. You must be happy to see your kids when they walk through the door. You need to initiate play time with your children. Sometimes you have to break the routine and just play around—lighten up and enjoy your children's company. Whether it's dancing, wrestling, or having ice cream before dinner, it's therapeutic to relax a little and share some laughs on a normal weekday.

A positive attitude affects how children interact with others and also helps them see the good in situations. Kids who have a positive attitude are better adjusted. They can transition between situations more easily than others. They are more resilient when faced with difficulty. How do you help your children develop a positive attitude? By providing positive experiences at home and by modeling a positive attitude yourself.

A positive attitude doesn't mean you always need to have positive experiences. It is about having a positive outlook despite what happens. You can always reframe a negative experience into a positive one. For example:

Negative attitudes
- "I hate going to your sister's house. I'm not eating there anymore. She always makes comments about our kids, and it's never a good time."
- "I went to the supermarket, and they were out of milk. I'm done shopping there!"
- "I can't stand the block we live on; there's never any parking!"
- "I didn't have time to make dinner because you missed the bus, and I needed to pick you up from school. Next time if you want dinner, don't be so irresponsible."

Positive attitudes
- "Let's stay home this Friday night as a family. I want some catch-up time with the kids."
- "The supermarket didn't have milk today, but we don't really need it. I'll pick some up tomorrow."
- "We live on a block full of great neighbors, which means parking can be a problem, but it's worth it."
- "Who wants cereal for dinner tonight?"

A positive attitude is taught. We can't control our experiences, but we can control how we respond to them. I remember bumping into a mom who was on vacation with my family the week before. When I saw her at the market, I asked how her flight home was. She told me it was delayed until the next day. This mom has four kids under the age of six. "Oh my gosh!" I said. "That's horrible! What did you do?" I was shocked to hear her response.

"Actually," she said, "it was so crazy that we laughed and decided to extend our trip a few more days on a nearby island. We had a great time!" I wanted to ask how she managed with a suitcase full of dirty laundry and four babies, but I was so taken back by how she responded to that horrible situation that I stayed silent. She taught me a valuable lesson: Life is what you make of it. Got lemons? Make lemonade!

As parents, it's important to differentiate between temperament and moods. Some children are born with an upbeat personality and a naturally positive attitude. Others may be more reserved and introverted. That doesn't mean the child is "sucky." You need to accept your children for who they are—the whole package. Either way, you can model positivity and help your children express themselves in a way that reflects their feelings. What does that look like?

- "Honey, Mommy loves to make you happy. When you are feeling happy, can you show me? Maybe a smile or even some words will do it."
- "Honey, if you are feeling upset by something I said, I want to know it, so I can avoid making you feel embarrassed. Your feelings are important to me."
- "Your smile brightens my day."
- "Aren't I the funniest mom in the world? I see you holding back from laughing!"

That all said, if a child seems unhappy on a consistent basis, it may be necessary to seek professional guidance.

Quotes to Hold On To

"Our attitude toward life determines life's attitude toward us."
—Earl Nightingale (American radio personality, motivational speaker, and author)

"Life is what you make it. Always has been, always will be."
—Eleanor Roosevelt

"Your attitude, not your aptitude, will determine your altitude."
—Zig Ziglar (American author, salesman, and motivational speaker)

12

Appearance

Have you ever noticed that when women meet, the first thing they usually do is compliment each other on their appearance? Without even realizing, we are hyper-focused on people's looks. "Wow! You look great." "Your skin is incredible!" "You cut your hair!" "You look amazing! Did you lose weight?" Unfortunately, in today's culture, how we look, dress, and act determine a person's worth. When did the world change so drastically? Are we not smart enough to know that value doesn't come in the form of a sheen?

I have news for you. We're all guilty of contributing to this toxic culture that surrounds our children. Of course, complimenting others on their appearance is certainly not a crime. In fact, teaching our children to be nice to others is important. But there's a balance between hyper-focusing on looks and greeting others with basic kindness. When you place your emphasis on people's appearance, your kids will pick up on that and internalize it by placing importance on their own appearance. So, don't be surprised if you find yourself asking, "Why is my daughter obsessed with her weight?" "Why is my son buying such expensive clothing?" "Do haircuts really cost that much?" I get plenty of phone calls about this topic. Children are putting constant pressure on their parents to "buy them beauty." "But everyone has it!" "I'm not going to school without my hair done!" "I need my own car. I'm not picking up a girl in your GMC, Mom."

When my grandparents were my age or a little older, I lived in their house during the summer. In our small community, everyone basically knew each other, and my grandparents always took me with them on their local errands. I vividly remember the conversations that took place whenever we saw their neighbors on the street. They asked each other three questions: "How are your parents doing?" "How are the children doing?" "What are your plans for the day?" Then they wished each other well and moved on. That was it.

The truth is, if you want your children to feel beautiful and have true self-esteem, you must look in the mirror—literally and figuratively. How much emphasis do you place on your own appearance? Is there a scale in the middle of the bathroom? Do you stare at the lines on your forehead? Do you buy clothes that you cannot afford? I am talking to myself, too. We all want to look our best. We want to look younger and more beautiful. The problem is, we will never be content because our culture will never allow us to be happy with our appearance. Why? Because we are surrounded by social media influencers and companies that tell us what we should look like and how they can help us achieve that image. I have six hundred wrinkle creams and treatments in my closet. I swore by each of them, and, lo and behold, I look the same. Now I wonder why my oldest daughter, who is thirteen with crystal-clear skin, is asking for a face cleanser. Her asking that question showed me the importance of writing this chapter.

Can you imagine the pressures your children are facing to look perfect? They are so exposed to this toxic culture that even when you parent well, you will never be able to fully shield them from the messages they see and hear on a daily basis. Even if you monitor their social media, they will struggle with insecurity. It's in the air, in the atmosphere in which they are growing up. Apparently, the young girls on YouTube who our children look up to never went through those "awkward" adolescent transitions. Their makeup always looks professionally done, and they never have a bad hair day. I'm sure I am not alone when I say that this was *not* the norm in my generation. What happened to looking back at high school pictures and cringing? Who else wore their sibling's shorts to camp, folded over multiple times because they didn't fit? Did anyone else carry gel in their school bag because there was no such thing as organic de-frizz hair treatments? We had it rough, didn't we? But we made it through. In fact, I believe we were actually better off. It was OK to be imperfect.

So, what to do? As always, it starts with us, the parents. Even with all the outside influences, remember that parents play a critical role in how children feel about themselves. It's your job to change your focus to allow yourself to age gracefully, love yourself (with all of your "flaws"), and see the beauty in everyone and everything. The way you see yourself is the first step toward teaching your children how to view themselves. When you see your body as beautiful, miraculous, and sacred, your children will begin to value theirs. The message is, *We aren't objects; we are people.*

When you influence your children in this way, you set the foundation for enduring self-esteem and self-worth. You help support a culture that focuses on true value so that your children can grow up to be self-loving, healthy individuals. When you see someone on the street, look deeper. Greet them with kindness, and make small talk about the real stuff—the stuff that actually holds value. "Nice to see you! How's your family?" "I heard your father is feeling better. I'm so happy to hear that." "Your daughter is so kind. She held the door for us when we were leaving the supermarket."

When my husband and I were first married, a relative stayed at my house for a night. I remember thinking what a beautiful girl she was, inside and out. After a long day at college, I came home and jumped in the shower. When I came out dressed in my husband's sweatshirt and bleach-stained sweatpants, she looked at me with her big blue eyes and beautiful face and said, "Wow, I wish I could look like you." I stared back at her and asked, "Do you know what you look like?" I didn't understand. In my eyes she was one of the prettiest girls I knew. But it didn't matter what I thought; she could not see her own beauty. I learned an important lesson that day. You can be the most beautiful person in the room and only see your flaws. The saying "Beauty lies in the eyes of the beholder" hits home when you see it firsthand.

Aside from throwing your scale out the window—or at least hiding it—you need to teach your children to be comfortable in their skin and feel an innate sense of confidence. This confidence comes from knowing that G-d created us exactly the way we should be, and in G-d's eyes, we are all created perfectly. Physical beauty is a façade, a sheen. That is why beauty is subjective. Have you ever met a person who didn't seem physically attractive to you at first, but after getting to know them, you saw the person as beautiful? Likewise, have you ever met someone who you saw as gorgeous, but after getting to know them, you no longer found them attractive? Inner beauty will always outshine physical beauty. It's no contest.

As a parent, it's your job to emphasize your children's inner beauty. Teach them not to rely on physical beauty to feel good about themselves and live a meaningful life. Every soul has a spiritual purpose that needs focus and direction. Aging reminds us to avoid getting attached to physical appearance. Children see what is in front of them. They pick up on the most subtle of gestures. They need to be taught the true definition of beauty. "But Norma," you may ask, "how realistic is that when my child comes to me and says she wishes she were thinner?" It's true that we live in a tough world, and it is naïve to think that our children will not face insecurity. In such moments, we are called to reassure our children that true beauty shines from within, that even the biggest celebrities face the same pressures and doubts. We are all human. Keep the dialogue open about purpose and true confidence. Don't tell your children they are the most beautiful or handsome kids in the world. That's an empty compliment. Everyone, including children, wants to be acknowledged on a deeper level and valued as a human being. In the chapter "The Orchestra," I discussed how children need to know their roles: how they contribute to this world with their goodness. Our physical appearance is only the vessel that takes us through our spiritual journey through life.

I recently planted a vegetable and herb garden. A friend of mine came by to give me a few tips on how to care for it. She told me, for example, to focus on the roots and not so much on the outer leaves when watering. *That makes sense*, I thought. If we only water the surface, the roots will not be able to properly nourish the plant. When it comes to parenting, remember to water the soul, not just the body.

How to Approach the Topic of Body Image

Whether you're currently struggling to help your children with body insecurity or a brand-new parent, the next few tips apply to all.

- **Start the conversation at an early age.** Studies show that children as young as age three worry about being overweight. Don't dismiss that conversation. If your child express concern about his or her weight, do not say, "You're crazy! You're beautiful." Instead, ask *why* your child thinks he or she is overweight. Steer the conversation toward how a healthy body doesn't always come in one size or one form.

- **Watch how you talk about** *your* **body.** The way you talk about your body will influence your children. Avoid discussing diets. Don't compare yourself to others: "I wish I looked like her." "Ugh, I ate two doughnuts' today!" "I can't eat that!"
- **Don't comment on either other people's bodies or, more importantly, your child's body.** If you notice that your child has gained weight, keep quiet. Period.
- **Smile when you look in the mirror.** Children pick up on how you see yourself.
- **Model healthy eating habits and exercise.** Lead by example when it comes to health and wellness.
- **Educate your children on outside pressures and unrealistic images.** Most of the images you see have been Photoshopped. Most models and celebrities have had work done: plastic surgery, Botox, and fillers. It's all fake news! Ask your children, "What makes this person beautiful? Does their personality play a role in how you see them?" Let them answer, then go on. "There's nothing wrong with being beautiful, but remember: they, too, will age, and they won't always be able to rely on their looks. I hope they've been using their platform to inspire people in a meaningful and purposeful way." I remember watching one of my favorite classic movies with my daughter. I told her that one of the actresses was considered one of the most beautiful women of my time. I opened my phone to show her a recent picture, and my daughter laughed and said, "Really? She's not that pretty, Ma." I took that opportunity to teach her a life lesson on beauty.
- **Let your children decide what they should eat.** Never say "no" to an older child when it comes to food choices. Studies show that depriving children of unhealthy foods and snacks will likely lead to unhealthy eating habits. With toddlers and children, allow unhealthy choices in moderation. As most parents likely know, allow toddlers and children to eat snacks all day, and they definitely will. That's why you need to put some boundaries in place. The goal is to find a healthy balance. Monitor unhealthy groceries that you keep in the home, and educate your children about the importance of fruit and vegetables. If family members or friends make comments on your child's food choices or eating habits, it's important to intervene. Address the person privately and respectfully and say, "We are making an effort to allow Sarah

to learn to trust her own body and decide what is best for her. Thanks for understanding."

- **If you have concerns about your children developing a poor body** image, seek professional help.

When Should Appearance Be a Focus?

The only time to emphasize appearance is when a child is not dressed properly. As parents, we have an obligation to teach our children to dress and act with *derekh eretz*: common decency, consideration, etiquette, and proper manners. An example of the opposite would be when someone is laughing among people who are weeping or attending a funeral wearing a slinky dress. In short, when your children aren't being sensitive to the feelings of others or considering your own reputation. *Derekh eretz* is not about taste; it's about a certain standard. It's up to you to decide what that standard is for your family. At the same time, allow space for individuality and independence.

"But Norma, what if my child wants to wear risqué clothing to a party?" Time for an intervention. "Your outfit is not in line with our values. In this family, it is not appropriate to dress in such a way."

"But everyone is wearing this!" your child may reply. Validate your child's feelings, but still enforce the rules.

"These are our values. We walk our own path. You are my child, and I don't care what other families say."

Quotes to Hold On To

"I am much more than what meets the eye. If you want to see the real me, you'll have to look deeper."
—Gilah Manolson (best-selling author of books on relationships and self-image)

"Beauty is how you feel inside, and it reflects in your eyes. It is not something physical."
—Sophia Loren

"Outer beauty pleases the eye. Inner beauty captivates the heart."
—Mandy Hale (author, blogger, and creator of the social media movement, the Single Woman)

PART IV: THE OUTSIDE WORLD

13

Balance

What does "finding balance" in our lives mean? It sounds beautiful, doesn't it? When people talk about "balance," they usually mean meeting two (or more!) goals at the same time that seem to interfere with each other. For example, exercising self-care while being productive is one way of living a balanced life. There is also the balance of juggling work and parenting responsibilities. One problem though: there is only so much a person can do in a day. No matter how many tips you get from friends or social media, finding that balance is not easy, and there is no fixed formula for fitting it all in. All too often, our daily to-do lists need to get done in a timely manner based on the needs of our kids and our jobs. For example, what happens when your child gets sick? While you might prefer to skip the doctor's office, you can't neglect their care, and working moms have deadlines to boot. This leads me to believe that a balanced life means getting it all done however you can with a smile.

Whether you're a working mom or a stay-at-home mom, parenting is hard. Even if a working mom has a great nanny, a mother carries the emotional stress of her kids 24/7. The moms who find balance usually focus their efforts on making their day-to-day routine run as efficiently as possible. They control what they can by scheduling their days and utilizing their time well. When time is an issue, they find ways to create more. They might wake up at 5 a.m., exercise at home, make a healthy shake, prepare dinner for the night, wake up the kids, make them a healthy breakfast, drive them to school, and get to work on time. Sounds insane, right? Even when everything works out as planned. Now let's talk about what a real morning looks like.

Mom wakes up after getting five hours of sleep, makes herself coffee, takes one sip, and then puts it on the counter. She wakes up the kids, pops a few waffles in the toaster, and makes three bagels with cream cheese for their lunches. She runs to make sure the kids are getting dressed and finds that her two-year-old had an accident that night. She throws the dirty sheets into the washing machine, grabs her now cold coffee, and while she's about to take a second sip, another child screams that he can't find his shoes. The clock is ticking. Mom finds his shoes exactly where they are supposed to be. She remembers the washed sheets and throws them in the dryer. She searches high and low for her coffee cup but can't remember where she left it. The kids are now ready for breakfast. Mom hands them each a waffle, but they want pancakes. She explains that they should have told her that earlier because there's no time to warm up the pancakes. "I'm not eating then!" She can't send them to school on an empty stomach, so she throws the pancakes in the microwave and hands them out on a paper towel to go. They finally get in the car, already a few minutes late, and, of course, the baby needs to use the bathroom. Welcome to Wednesday!

This may look and sound like a movie, but it's real life most mornings. On top of everything else, the mom usually feels guilty for everything she thinks she could have done better to have made the day start more smoothly.

If you can wake up earlier, have the kids' clothes already picked out from the day before and a breakfast menu that has met their approval along with preparing their lunches and snacks, kudos! But realistically, how many parents can be that organized the night before when they were busy with the nighttime routine and exhausted from a long day at work? Plus, how can parents account for all the unexpected complications that come up on any given day? As all parents know, it's impossible to plan for everything. Our days and nights are usually unpredictable, and somehow, children know how to find the most inconvenient times to throw us a curveball.

The solution to managing parenthood is to try to survive in the best way you can. Knowing you can't do it all, be easy on yourself. If mornings are harder for you, try finding some extra energy the night before. If nights are hard, save some things for the morning. My husband jokes that I'm not a morning *or* a night person, and he's right. I'm more of a three-hour midday kind of girl.

Take some comfort in the fact that each day's responsibilities *shouldn't* all fall on one person. If you have older children, delegate some tasks. Have a family meeting, and discuss sharing the work. Kids are blessed with a lot more energy than their parents. Maybe they'd like to prepare breakfast or make their own lunches for school. If one child is good at math, that child can help with schedules. Allow a child to wake the others up in the morning. The point is, get as much help as you can. Everyone is human, and the unpredictability of life and parenthood allows us to learn and grow every day. Accept the uncertainty and unpredictability of life, and try to embrace it.

Don't make the search for balance yet another goal on your to-do list. If there was an answer to having it all figured out, wouldn't we know it by now? I have a better suggestion. Put your energy into forming genuine connections with other parents and finding and sharing the proper support. In today's world, we often connect superficially through social media, leaving us feeling isolated and defeated. The world needs more human interaction and personal relationships for meaningful support. Keep an open dialogue with those around you, and be more realistic about what you can do and what you need help with. On my parenting journey, I've tossed finding balance into the garbage and replaced it with a more appropriate goal: finding the proper support.

In the meantime, stay away from the "perfectly balanced" mom accounts on social media. They are endless and represent distorted views of reality. "Onefunnymommy," a comedienne's Instagram account, talks about how parents should use social media as a platform to show the reality of parenthood, not the fluffy parts. "Everybody showing how they are Carol Brady . . . Why do not you show them when 'mommy dearest' comes out when you are climbing up those stairs with a trenched mouth foaming like a rottweiler. Get to bed!! Show that one! Show that part . . . Show when you get the lock jaw when your gonna lost it. Let us be real here, people . . . This is Instagram people it is a safe place. . . Let's show the truth." She's hilarious (and not grammatically "perfect"!) and she says it how it really is.

The following is a list of some basic self-care to help you ride out the storm when the kids get home.

- Rest before they arrive if you can manage to do so. If not, drink a cup of coffee. Don't worry; you'll quit when the kids get older.
- Don't greet them with an empty stomach. Eat something—anything—before they walk in.
- Change into comfortable clothing.
- Go to the bathroom.
- Turn up the radio on the way to picking your kids up from school, and sing your heart out.
- Disconnect from your phone.
- If dinner isn't ready, have some go-to snacks ready while you prepare.

You Time

One final tip to all the moms out there: take a few hours for yourself each month that you can look forward to. It will give you the strength and peace of mind that is necessary to get through all the rest. You deserve it.

Quotes to Hold On To

"The key is not to prioritize what's on your schedule, but to schedule your priorities."
—Stephen Covey (educator, author, businessman, and speaker)

"Forget work-life balance...Do the thing you want and create systems to support that. Perfectly imbalanced in the direction you want to go is perfectly acceptable."
—Richie Norton (author, coach, speaker, entrepreneur)

"The fastest way to break the cycle of perfectionism and become a fearless mother is to give up the idea of doing it perfectly—indeed, to embrace uncertainty and imperfection."
—Arianna Huffington

14

Diagnoses

I went back and forth about whether to address the issue of diagnoses because I am not a psychologist. I ultimately decided that a person doesn't need a PhD in psychology to share thoughts about topics with which they have personal experience. The symptoms of ADHD (attention-deficit/hyperactivity disorder) in particular hit close to home, and through experience I have gained insight into how it presents and how to manage it.

I have received so many calls over the years from parents who open up to me about children who are having difficulties, and the possibility of ADHD (originally called ADD) is often ringing in my head. And no wonder: ADHD is one of the most prevalent mental health diagnoses for children (along with depression and anxiety). Almost 10 percent of children meet the criteria for this disorder at some point in their young lives, with boys twice as likely to be diagnosed as girls. Whenever I introduce the possibility of ADHD to a parent, the response is usually the same: "But my child is very smart." "But my child isn't hyper." "But my child can play video games for two hours." "Oh, it's definitely not that." Mental health challenges are often misunderstood and, unfortunately, still very much stigmatized. Many children with ADHD who fall through the cracks could have benefited tremendously from an appropriate diagnosis. When parents tell me, "It doesn't matter. I refuse to medicate my child," I always reply with, "Knowledge is power," reminding them that medication is not always the answer.

A Life-Changing Experience

There are many benefits to knowing if your child has a mental health disorder. I am focusing on ADHD because it's so prevalent and because I have firsthand knowledge of it. Being clear on a diagnosis allows parents to work with their children within a useful framework. Knowing what their children are struggling with can help parents teach their children the skills they need to manage symptoms that don't require medication. For example, you can teach your children to focus, organize themselves, control their impulses, and manage their time. Whether you take the route of medication, seek alternative strategies, or are at the stage of getting an education about your child's condition, it can be a life-changing experience for both of you.

For example, when parents learn their child has ADHD, they can become their child's advocate by keeping an open dialogue with teachers, discussing the child's struggles and different ways of supporting the children throughout the day. Maybe it's a fidget spinner, chewing gum, or incorporating a three-minute exercise program that can be used throughout the day. Homework time can be a more positive experience for parents and children by throwing the words "sit down" out the window and replacing them with "Jumping jacks!" Sometimes the smallest adjustments can turn a negative experience into a positive one. Children with disabilities have a more challenging time, and when a parent is able to understand their children's needs and support them according to those needs, it brings a special closeness to their relationship.

What to Look for

We can all guess what the "typical" profile of a child with ADHD looks like, but there are "not so typical" symptoms as well. Here is a pretty complete list of all symptoms.

- Lack of focus/easily distracted
- Fidgety
- Impulsive
- Unable to finish tasks
- Difficulty playing quietly
- Talking excessively
- Impatient
- Trouble moving from task to task (transitioning)
- Difficulty self-regulating emotions
- Avoidance of difficult tasks that require effort
- Lack of organizational skills
- Staring into space (daydreaming)
- Wandering
- Forgetful
- Lacking time-management skills
- Difficulty paying attention to detail
- Making careless mistakes
- Difficulty following directions
- Focusing only on tasks they enjoy

Children can struggle with any combination of these characteristics. Some struggle primarily with attention. Others are impulsive, and still others may be inattentive and impulsive/hyperactive.

Evaluating children is a fairly new concept that has become a popular parenting approach. There are some who say it has gone too far and that we are overanalyzing and over-diagnosing children who don't necessarily need treatment. There is some truth to that, and I agree there needs to be some level of tolerance when it comes to children's behavior without jumping to classifying them as "impaired." I can also understand those who say that some parents are looking for a "quick fix" and a diagnosis to validate their struggles with the child. On the other hand, early intervention can make a tremendous difference in a child's life, and it's imperative not to avoid a problem that can become bigger over time. So, proceed cautiously.

A few years ago, after going through a traumatic experience, I went to a psychiatrist for help. I was a little hesitant because I thought I knew pretty much everything about myself and what I was experiencing. Soon after I started the first session, I realized I was wrong. Not only did we discuss my immediate issue, after a few minutes of talking about myself, the doctor told me that I have ADHD! I was one of those kids who fell through the cracks. He said if he were to give me an IQ test, I would score strongly, but alongside my strong reasoning, I was struggling with attention. When I left his office, I started to cry in my car. The tears weren't only about the trauma we had discussed but the validation that the little girl inside of me finally felt understood. That's when I decided to start writing. I finally had the confidence to think about going back to school and becoming a psychologist one day. During our next session, I told the doctor about my new project (this book) and how I started giving parenting classes. He was beaming with pride. He told me that he wasn't surprised because I was not his only patient who, after learning of their disability, moved on to do incredible things.

Upon hearing of my diagnosis, my husband said, "But you turned out pretty damn good." I answered that I still wish I had known. Maybe I wouldn't have chosen a different path in life, but the knowledge would have given me the confidence to know I had options. Maybe I would have explored my passions early on by taking classes at college that actually interested me. My insights begged a question: if someone (like me) who didn't suffer tremendously without such knowledge still would have wanted to know, how many children who suffer from ADHD or other challenging diagnoses would want the option of intervention? How many of those children who grow into adults would have led a different life if the adults around them knew why they were struggling and how to help them? Would they have led a happier life? Would they have become more successful?

In so many cases, intervention is necessary. Gambling on possible lifelong struggles is not a bet I would take. My advice is to trust the process. That doesn't mean we need to run to medicate or rely solely on a "diagnosis" for the final word. On the contrary, it means we get more information from which to make choices. It's best to get as much clarity as you can. If you are on the fence about getting your child evaluated, I say yes, yes, and yes! Give your children all the support they need, so they can reach their full potential. As parents, let's educate ourselves, weigh our options, rely on our intuition, and do the best we can.

I would love to speak to other important diagnoses, but I'm just not qualified. All I can say is there are experts in these fields who can provide the education and guidance you are looking for. My goal for this chapter has been to stress the importance of being proactive about seeking guidance and support. My psychologist friend says that not having knowledge of what you are dealing with is like throwing darts at a dart board in the dark. If you are on the path of seeking insight for a child's emotional, behavioral, or developmental issue, set up a consultation appointment with a clinical psychologist or psychiatrist to get some diagnostic clarity. If there is a diagnosis, it's important to know as early as possible. If they rule something out, that is equally valuable to know. Either way, it will allow you to make informed choices about treatment, come up with an effective and specific plan of action, and, most importantly, parent your children according to their individual needs.

Quotes to Hold On To

"Knowledge is power. Information is liberating. Education is the premise of progress, in every society, in every family."
—Kofi Annan (Nobel Peace Prize laureate and former secretary general of the United Nations)

"I failed in some subjects in exam, but my friend passed in all. Now he is an engineer for Microsoft, and I am the owner of Microsoft."
—Bill Gates

"Everybody is a genius. But if you judge a fish by its ability to climb a tree, it will live its whole life believing that it is stupid."
—Albert Einstein

15

Sacrifice

"Nothing in this world is worth having or worth doing unless it means effort, pain, and difficulty... I have never in my life envied a human being who led an easy life. I have envied a great many people who led difficult lives and led them well."
—Theodore Roosevelt

"What you put into life is what you get out of it."
—Clint Eastwood

Although it may seem that your efforts go unnoticed by your kids, your role is unappreciated, and your days are full of mundane tasks, make no mistake, like all things of value, the investment in parenting is worth it. I have learned that fulfillment creeps up on parents in a subtle way.

Parenthood is anything but ordinary, but ironically, it is filled with tasks that are routine and at times feel empty. My parenting teacher, Esther, taught me a valuable lesson. Every task can be looked at as ordinary or important; it is the individual who drives it to purpose. Every diaper change, every bath, every meal, every smile, every pee pee accident, every argument, every carpool, every single effort you put into your children can be viewed as mundane or purposeful. Why does it matter? Because with a shift in focus, the importance of your role is highlighted. After all, you are raising human beings! That perspective should anchor you, embrace you, guide you, and carry you through the trials and triumphs of parenting.

Raising children is challenging. It's the most demanding job in the world. All the physical and emotional sacrifices of parenthood can never be measured. Are they worth it? You bet. I believe children enrich and illuminate the world. I also believe that fulfillment comes from hard work and sacrifice. Life is a process of growth, and parenthood can encourage us to become our best selves. I believe that givers get more than receivers and that giving unto others leads to true happiness. I believe that bringing children into this world is a gift from above and a gift for future generations.

Special Thanks

Rabbi Yisroel Salanter was asked once if he had studied under Rabbi Zundel of Salant, who was known to be his teacher. Rabbi Yisroel replied, "I did not study under him. I saw him. Just taking a careful look at his actions and habits were already an entire series of lessons in elevated behavior." (Rabbi Zelig Pliskin, from *Growth Through Torah*)

It is not coincidental that this quote stuck with me ever since I read it, and that I was able to type it without referring to it. It is also not coincidental that this quote is from the book that you, Mrs. Tawachi, gifted me over ten years ago.

Not only was I fortunate enough to have learned from you over the years, I was also fortunate enough to have been able to watch you. Thank you for being my teacher, my mentor, and my compass. I am truly blessed to be your student.

May Hashem continue to bless you with the wisdom, patience, and warmth to guide and teach our community. I love you.

About the Author

Born and raised in Brooklyn, New York, Norma Gindi is a friend, a neighbor, an ear to listen to and a shoulder to cry on. When she's not juggling the daily demands of raising four children--Vivian, Frieda, Eddy, and Ronnie--with her husband, Zac, she is offering her time and wise advice as a parenting coach and consultant to dozens of people in her community. This is her first book.

Made in the USA
Columbia, SC
25 June 2021